ENL ~~~~~~~~~~~

In this book, Russell Morris examines the postmodern context of the church by questioning whether or not we are being influenced by our culture. With the assumption that Christian character is based on the ethics of Jesus, Dr. Morris offers biblical principles for successful Christian living.

Jerry F. Chitwood
Church of God State Administrative Bishop
Western North Carolina

This book is not only excellent and insightful in content, but written by a man whose life has exemplified the principles about which he has written. Knowing Dr. Morris as a fellow minister and Christian friend, I do not believe he could have chosen a topic for his first book more indicative of his character and how he "lives" his own life for Jesus Christ.

Deborah V. Snodgrass, Ed.D., NCC, NCLPC
Online Faculty, Liberty University

Dr. Morris' book is certainly worth reading. He approaches the subject in a very straight-forward manner. The mixing of theology with the practicalities of life is well done.

Thomas L. Tatum, D.Min.
Pastor, Teacher, Educator

Here is stimulus for Christian behavior that will influence every follower of Christ. These pages are filled with hope and direction in fleshing out our faith.

Fred Killman
Pastor, Teacher, Educator

Christian Ethics

Where Life and Faith Meet

Russell A. Morris

WESTBOW®
PRESS
A DIVISION OF THOMAS NELSON
& ZONDERVAN

Unless otherwise indicated, all Scripture quotations are taken from the Holy Bible, New International Version®. NIV®. Copyright © 1973, 1978, 1984 by the International Bible Society. Used by permission of Zondervan. All rights reserved.

Verses marked NASB are taken from the New American Standard Bible®. Copyright © 1960, 1962, 1963, 1968, 1971, 1972, 1973, 1975, 1977 The Lockman Foundation. Used by permission. All rights reserved.

Verses marked NLT are taken from the Holy Bible, New Living Translation, copyright © 1996, 2004. Used by permission of Tyndale House Publishers, Inc., Wheaton, IL 60189 USA. All rights reserved.

WestBow Press books may be ordered through booksellers or by contacting:

WestBow Press
A Division of Thomas Nelson & Zondervan
1663 Liberty Drive
Bloomington, IN 47403
www.westbowpress.com
1 (866) 928-1240

ISBN: 978-1-4908-9263-4 (sc)

Print information available on the last page.

WestBow Press rev. date: 08/04/2015

To My Girls

My Wife
Wanda Millard Morris

My Daughter
Nichole Squires

My Granddaughters
Hope, Brianna & McKamie Squires

Acknowledgements

- To Dr. Noel Woodbridge, postgraduate supervisor in practical theology at the South African Theological Seminary, under whose supervision this book was originally written as a thesis for the master of theology in practical theology degree.

- To Dr. Hendrik J. C. Pieterse, emeritus professor of practical theology at the University of South Africa, who served as the external reader for the original thesis.

- To the leadership, staff and parishioners of Harvest Hills Church, who have allowed me the distinct privilege to serve as senior pastor since May 1, 2000. The content of the original thesis was used as the basis for a series of sermons. This book is the culmination of both.

- To Mrs. Bonnie Davis, church secretary and retired English teacher, who proofread the entire manuscript. I am indebted to her for offering grammatical and editing expertise—both of which proved invaluable.

Contents

FOREWORD

It is so refreshing to find a book that reminds us—without being dogmatic—that there are lifestyle requirements for Christian living. In a church world where almost every person confesses to be a Christian, the words of James 1:23-24 are profoundly relevant. *Anyone who listens to the word but does not do what it says is like a man who looks at his face in a mirror and, after looking at himself, goes away and immediately forgets what he looks like* (NIV).

In this book, Dr. Russell A. Morris examines the theological background for Christian ethics. He reminds us that our faith must dictate our actions. Many are strong in faith, yet weak in following up with a consistent Christian lifestyle. God has given an awakening almost every fifty years that stirred the church concerning a laxity of Christian ethics. Perhaps God sees our plight and will give us a spiritual awakening.

This book tells us where we are and how important Christian ethics is to our society. One can feel the heartbeat of the author. Hopefully, it will also touch the heart of the reader. One cannot read this book without being academically challenged and spiritually inspired.

Bill F. Sheeks, D.Min.

INTRODUCTION

Within the Christian community at large there is often little correlation between scriptural guidelines for Christian living and the lifestyle practices and behavior of believers. Christian social scientist, George Barna, has done extensive research in this area that reveals alarming data. For example, nearly nine of ten adults state that religious faith is very important in their lives. However, only one in five adults claims that the Bible is the dominant influence in their decisions regarding lifestyle practices.[1] Further research suggests that there is often little difference between the lifestyle practices of Christians and non-Christians.[2] This nominal difference in lifestyle practices and behavior between Christians and non-Christians, as well as the minimal correlation between Scripture and practice among many Christians, produced an interest in this area of practical theology.

Apathy is a dominant trait within the church of the 21st century. This is evident not only in a diminished zeal for evangelism but also in the lack of commitment to biblical guidelines in determining behavioral and lifestyle practices. Partial responsibility lies within the context of postmodernism, characterized by its rejection of absolute truth. In postmodernism, truth is defined by and for the community, not by an established objective standard.[3] A majority vote of approval on a given issue seems to be the pattern adopted by many Christians. If everyone is doing it, whatever *it* may be, then it must be acceptable.

Many have begun to piece together a customized version of the faith that borrows liberally from any available and appealing faith.[4]

Serving as a Christian pastor over the past two decades, the reality of Barna's research has been observed personally. The biblical parallel of the prevailing apathy within today's churches is seen in Judges 21:25 (NASB), *In those days there was no king in Israel, everyone did what was right in his own eyes.* That is, in those days there was no accepted standard of truth. Likewise, only one in four American adults believes in the existence of absolute truth.[5] As a result, the relationship between doctrine and practice, belief and behavior, is often minimal, with many Christians doing only what *is right in their own eyes*, rather than allowing God's Word to influence their mode of living.

A distinct relationship between belief and behavior is seen in I Timothy 4:16. In this passage, Paul clearly identifies a correlation between what one believes (doctrine) and the lifestyle (behavior) one lives when he writes, *Watch your life and doctrine closely. Persevere in them, because if you do, you will save both yourself and your hearers.* From this verse it is clear that there are two areas in the life of the Christian that need to be scrutinized and pursued, namely, belief and behavior. The fundamental thesis of this book is that a deeper understanding of Christian ethics will inform and facilitate the Christian life.

PART ONE

EXPLORING THE FRAMEWORK

CHAPTER ONE

A Survey Relating to the Christian Lifestyle

The pastoral role is designed to prepare God's people to become mature for the purpose of attaining to the whole measure of the fullness of Christ (Ephesians 4:10-13). Becoming a mature Christian requires spiritual growth. To achieve this objective the pastor is to be both a model and a mentor. By virtue of his position the pastor serves as a model for Christian living. Paul instructs Timothy as a Christian pastor to set an example for the believers in speech, in life, in love, in faith and in purity (I Timothy 4:12). The pastor's life is to be characterized by a sincere faith, a good conscience, a godly lifestyle, and purity of heart. Spiritual maturity modeled by the pastor is essential for promoting spiritual growth. The pastor is also a mentor. In this capacity the pastor is in a strategic position to influence the belief and behavior of parishioners.

For the past two decades, I have served in the pastorate. During this time I have observed firsthand that there is often minimal correlation between biblical guidelines for Christian living and the lifestyle practices of Christians. Examples include but are not limited to: 1) a general lack of commitment to spiritual matters; 2) little or no involvement in impacting the culture for Christ; 3) a lack of emphasis on issues of personal integrity; and, in recent years, 4) a noticeable decrease in emphasis on matters of moral purity. Unfortunately, there is no deficit of persons who struggle with living an exemplary Christian life.

Extensive research has been conducted among Evangelicals regarding spiritual growth, Christian behavior and lifestyle issues. Numerous sources[6] were utilized to help determine the need for promoting, encouraging and facilitating the Christian lifestyle. A survey[7] was conducted within my current church[8] to gain a better understanding of the need for an effective model of Christian ethics. In this brief chapter, based on the findings of the survey, the following areas are examined: 1) the impact of worldviews on one's commitment to Christian living; 2) challenges to spiritual growth; and 3) feedback from survey participants regarding lifestyle issues.

Negative Worldviews

The survey was designed to obtain information regarding the negative impact of specific worldviews on one's commitment to living a Christian lifestyle.[9] Participants in the survey were asked to rate the following worldviews in terms of their perceived negative impact on Christian lifestyles and behavior. Each worldview is listed below, along with the percentage of persons who perceived the worldview as a challenge to effectively integrating belief and behavior.

(1)   Materialism (78%)
The only thing that really matters in life is the accumulation of things. Life's highest values lie in material well-being and the things one possesses.

(2)   Individualism (76%)
This is a self-centered, individualistic way of life that suggests one should ignore the community and other people, because all values and rights originate in the individual.

(3)   Hedonism (75%)
The ultimate goal and objective in life is happiness and pleasure, to feel good, be comfortable, have fun and be entertained.

(4)   Humanism (74%)
A special value is assigned to human beings and their activities and achievements. Because life is centered on human values, there is no need for God.

(5)   Pragmatism (73%)
It doesn't matter if a behavior is wrong or right or whether or not it hurts anyone. Everything in life is determined by its practicality.

(6)   Atheism (67%)
This is a rejection of belief in God. Because God does not exist, I am an accident of nature and my life has no value, meaning or purpose.

A brief examination of the results indicates that each of the six worldviews was perceived as having a negative impact on the Christian's commitment to living according to Christian ethics. Although perceptions varied in each category, the average percentage for each worldview gave it a negative impact rating from 67% to 78%. The worldview with the highest perceived negative impact was materialism (78%), which corresponds with the current cultural emphasis in this area. This could also be said of the other worldviews, which seem to indicate that certain facets of contemporary culture do indeed have a negative impact on applying a Christian ethic to one's life. As a result, there is often little emphasis on the importance of spiritual growth and maturity.

Since one's worldview does indeed have an impact, either positively or negatively, on how one integrates belief and behavior, the results reveal the need to emphasize and encourage a biblical worldview among believers.

Challenges to Spiritual Growth

Spiritual growth is necessary for the ongoing integration of belief and behavior in one's life. When spiritual growth occurs, the believer engages the process of maturity—the desired pattern of Christian living described in Scripture. In this part of the survey, participants were asked to rate lifestyle areas in which they were challenged regarding spiritual growth. The survey focused on seven key aspects relating to a Christian lifestyle and behavior, with each offering biblically based guidelines for practical Christian living.[10]

Each of the following seven areas is important to one's spiritual growth and development, therefore, warranting emphasis. Each area is listed below along with the percentage of persons who perceived the category to have challenges to spiritual growth, and who had personally experienced those challenges:

(1)   Example (84%)
Demonstrating one's commitment to Christ through the practice of the spiritual disciplines, to the body of Christ through loyalty to God and the church, and to the work of Christ through good stewardship

(2)   Purity (76%)
Committing to engage in those activities which glorify God in one's body and which avoid the fulfillment of the lust of the flesh, including reading, watching and listening to those things which are of positive benefit to one's spiritual well being

(3)   Integrity (69%)
Living in a manner that inspires trust and confidence, bearing the fruit of the Spirit and seeking to manifest the character of Christ in all behavior

(4)   Self-Control (45%)
Practicing self-control in behavior and abstaining from activities and attitudes offensive to one's peers and addictive in nature

(5)   Community (45%)
Fulfilling our obligations to society by being good citizens, correcting social injustices, and protecting the sanctity of life

(6) Etiquette (35%)
Demonstrating the scriptural principle of modesty by appearing and dressing in a manner that will enhance one's Christian testimony and will avoid pride or sensuality

(7) Family (31%)
Giving priority to family responsibilities, preserving the sanctity of marriage and maintaining divine order in the home

The survey revealed that certain areas presented challenges regarding spiritual growth. These findings correspond to a large extent with today's general cultural and religious climate. In particular, the findings correlate with research that found 74% of parishioners from orthodox and independent churches believe that current moral values are weaker than they were twenty years ago.[11] This supports the notion that certain facets of culture do indeed have a negative impact on Christian behavior.

Feedback from Participants

In the third section of the survey, participants were asked to reflect on the guidelines for Christian living listed above, and to rank the top four problematic areas. Feedback was requested concerning noticeable symptoms in each area, answering the question, "What traits do you see in yourself or others that suggest this area is a challenge to spiritual growth?" Following is the ranking and a sampling of the responses:

(1) Example
- Taking spiritual growth lightly
- Apathy regarding church attendance
- Lack of faithful stewardship
- Lack of involvement in ministry

(2) Purity
- The influence of television and media
- Yielding to carnal temptations

- The influence of the world
- Negative lifestyle of some Christians

(3) Integrity
- Negative influence of culture
- Lack of consistent Christian living
- Lack of faithful church attendance
- Selfish desire to better one's self

(4) Self-Control
- Uncontrolled carnal behavior
- Addictions among some Christians
- Hidden sins, wrong attitudes and criticism
- Influence of carnal vices

Clearly, the survey revealed several important details. First, there is a need among Christians in general to understand and apply a biblical worldview in matters of life and faith. Second, ongoing spiritual growth is an essential component to living an exemplary Christian life. Third, because challenges do exist in integrating belief and behavior, guidelines for practical Christian living are needed.

Successfully living the Christian life is no easy task. Challenges abound. Several biblical passages suggest that it will become even more challenging as our Lord's return draws near. However, the Bible assures success in this area by offering power for living.

Chapter Two

The Church in a Postmodern World

This chapter focuses on the contemporary context of the church. The discipline of practical theology involves assisting the world to become what God intends it to be. However, to contribute in a meaningful way to God's intended purpose for the world, one must first understand the world as it is. For the church in the 21st century this means an understanding of postmodernism. Within this context, those who comprise the church face unique challenges in applying a biblical ethic to matters of lifestyle and personal behavior.

In brief, postmodernism is a rejection of and reaction to the basic tenets of modernism. This is especially true regarding the acceptance of absolute truth. This reaction to modernism results in a worldview that embraces *anything, everything and nothing.*[12]

> Today, all the major ideological constructions are being tossed on the ash heap of history. All that remains is the cynicism of postmodernism, with its false assertions that there is no objective truth or meaning, that we are free to create our own truth.[13]

To gain a better understanding of this context the following subjects are discussed: 1) the state of the contemporary church; and 2) the context of the contemporary church.

The State of the Contemporary Church

Through the venue of a novel, Charles Dickens describes the cultural and social upheaval of his time:

> It was the best of times, it was the worst of times, it was the age of wisdom, it was the age of foolishness, it was the epoch of belief, it was the epoch of incredulity, it was the season of Light, it was the season of Darkness, it was the spring of hope, it was the winter of despair, we had everything before us, we had nothing before us.[14]

Dickens' description adequately depicts much of contemporary culture and to some extent the church as well. In recent decades, the church has undergone dramatic change, much of which is the result of shifting trends in culture.

Contemporary Trends in Society

Today's society has myriad complex components. The population is becoming increasingly secularized in its orientation, as well as fragmented on many levels. During the past two-three decades, numerous changes have taken place, each contributing to the increasing diversity within society at large. The following statistical data addresses societal trends within American culture; however, these trends serve to underscore the general nature of ever-changing societies.

The ethnicity of the United States alone is becoming increasingly diverse. By the year 2050, it is projected that minority groups will comprise 50% of the total 420 million population, with Hispanics comprising 25%, African Americans 15%, and Asians 8%.[15] During this same time period, the non-Hispanic white population is projected to comprise just 50% of the total population. The trend toward an ever-expanding ethnicity is a significant factor in the changing demographics of society.

Ours is a nation of both extreme wealth and dismal poverty. At the turn of the 21st century the United States was home to 276 billionaires, over 2,500 households with a net worth exceeding $100 million, 350,000 persons with a net worth of $10 million, and 5 million millionaires.[16] The disproportionate levels of wealth have produced a culture of those who have and those who do not have. The middle class is shrinking as the rich are becoming super rich, increasing inflated expectations and overly pampered lifestyles.[17] Ironically, many seem oblivious to these inflated expectations, assuming a posture of socio-economic entitlement. The result of such self-indulgence is that many are drowning in debt.

In terms of education, former United States Attorney General Robert Bork writes that the United States spends more on education than do other Western industrialized nations but gets less in return.[18] With such massive amounts of money funding public education, one would expect better return rates. However, Bork's assessment appears to be accurate. In the past several decades, school violence has escalated, while academic standards have declined. In 1997 alone over one million students were allowed to graduate high school, even though they could not read their diploma.[19]

Technological advances over the past several decades have transformed the dynamics of society. The rapid escalation and incorporation of e-mail, facsimiles, Internet, online distance education, mass computerization, etc., continue to introduce seismic change within society at large. It appears that this trend will continue to escalate, creating both innovative consumer items and critical challenges.

Perhaps no demographic area is experiencing more seismic transition than the family. Statistically, fewer adults are getting married, more are divorced or remaining single, more are living together outside of marriage, more children are born out-of-wedlock, and more are living in stepfamilies, with cohabiting but unmarried adults, or with a single parent. The trend of redefining the concept of family can only add to the ever-growing challenges facing society in the twenty-first century. This brief sampling of trends within American society at large serves to contextualize the trends occurring within the church.

Contemporary Trends in the Church

Just as society is experiencing trends that produce change, so too is the church. Although many exhibit a broad and pervasive faith, it is not always a deep faith.[20] The lack of depth among many Christians contributes to the overall context of the church.

From its inception America has been immersed in a religious context. While revisionist historians often minimize the importance of the Christian faith—specifically the church—in the birth and development of this nation, a brief perusal of history reveals otherwise. As the first decade of the twenty-first century approaches closure, three developments are shaping the church: 1) while conservative churches are growing, mainline church membership is in decline; 2) political activism seriously divides mainline churches; and 3) a radical separation of church and state contributes to the secularization of society.[21]

The Hartford Institute for Religion Research estimates there are approximately 335,000 religious congregations in America, with between 20-40% of the population attending worship on a given Sunday.[22] Of those, about 300,000 are Protestant churches, with 22,000 being Catholic and Orthodox churches. Non-Christian religious congregations are estimated at about 12,000. Of these 335,000 churches, the median church has 75 regular participants in worship on Sunday. However, while there is indeed a large number of very small churches, most people attend the larger churches. It is estimated that the smaller churches draw only about 11% of those who attend worship. Meanwhile, 50% of churchgoers attend 10% of the largest congregations. A brief examination of churches by size will be helpful at this point.

House Churches

Biblical precedent for the house church concept is found in several New Testament passages. In Romans 16:3-5, Paul writes:

> Greet Priscilla and Aquila, my fellow workers in Christ Jesus. They risked their lives for me. Not only I but all the churches of the Gentiles are grateful to them. Greet also *the church that meets at their house* [Italics added].

A house church is defined as a group of believers who meet in a home or some other informal setting, tending to be small, comprised of between six to thirty people. Also known as organic churches or simple churches, these small communities of faith meet in homes, offices, campuses, wherever the opportunity arises.

House churches are becoming more and more common. Their attractiveness is due in part to the intimate nature of a smaller setting. One out of every ten adults participates in a house church in a typical week, with a similar number attending once per month.[23] This trend will likely continue, as the number of house church attendees is expected to double in the coming decade.

Small Churches

The small church is defined within broad parameters; however, an attendance of less than 100 in attendance offers a general guideline. Approximately 60% of all churches average 75 or less in weekly attendance, a percentage that holds true across racial and class boundaries.[24] Small churches remain attractive to constituents for numerous reasons. First, the smaller context often fosters more intimate relationships, a trait seen by many as necessary for spiritual formation. Second, while not always the case, many small churches continue to exist and thrive because of family heritage. Third, small churches are attractive for the level of participation and personal involvement per capita. Small churches do not appear to be in decline but continue to represent a sizable portion of the church market.

Mid-Size Churches

While both small and large churches are maintaining momentum and gaining constituents, the mid-size churches with an average attendance of 100-300 have experienced a minimal decline.[25] Several factors have contributed to this decline:

(1)   Many people begin to attend larger churches, believing they are upgrading to first class ministry

(2)   There are multiple expectations on mid-size churches that often cannot be met, such as dynamic cutting-edge music, innovative youth ministries, etc.

(3)   Mid-size churches simply do not possess the necessary financial resources to compete with their larger counterparts, which are an absolute necessity for providing the myriad ministries offered by larger churches

While the slight decrease in attendance has been noted, mid-size churches continue to impact their constituents and communities in very positive ways.

Large Churches

Large churches are alive and well. The growth of large churches, those averaging 300-2000 in attendance, is somewhat connected to the circulation of contemporary believers. Research reveals that most new attendees of larger churches used to attend smaller churches.[26] Many, if not most, larger churches have the financial resources and personnel to offer ministries that appeal to a wide range of constituents.

> These churches appeal to young families and have a wider range of congregational activities, ranging from peer groups for mothers of preschoolers to young adult basketball leagues to divorce recovery groups...A primary goal of these churches is numerical growth, which will enable them to expand their range of programs and to expand their facilities...One of the pastor's consistent challenges is to keep people focused on the vision and primary goals of the church.[27]

By virtue of growth, the large churches will no doubt continue to influence and impact today's religious context.

The Mega-Churches

Somewhat of an innovation during the past twenty to thirty years is the rapid increase in the number of mega-churches. According to the Hartford Institute there are currently over 1200 such churches in the United States.[28] The term mega-church is the name given to a cluster of very large congregations that share several distinctive characteristics. These churches generally have:

(1) 2000 or more persons in attendance at weekly worship
(2) A charismatic, authoritative senior minister
(3) A very active seven-days-a-week congregational community
(4) A multitude of social and outreach ministries
(5) A complex differentiated organizational structure[29]

Mega-churches, more so than their smaller counterparts, most often have the resources, both financial and personnel, to offer a variety of ministry opportunities. This ability only enhances their attraction. These churches will no doubt continue to increase in number and impact Christianity and culture at large.

Trends Changing the Religious Landscape

Today's religious landscape is in a state of flux and transition. At the turn of the twentieth century, most Americans observed religious expression within primarily a Judeo-Christian worldview. While other religious traditions were present, the dominant worldview was Judeo-Christian. However, by the turn of the twenty-first century, religious expression had shifted to include numerous belief systems. There are some interesting signs that the religious landscape continues in a state of rapid transition:

(1) The percentage of adults who identify themselves as Christians dropped from 86% in 1990 to 77% in 2001. This is an unprecedented drop of almost 1 percentage point per year.

(2) The percentage of adults who identify themselves as Protestants dropped below 50% about the year 2005.

(3) Confidence in religious institutions has hit an all-time low.

(4) There appears to be a major increase of interest in spirituality. However, this has not translated into greater church involvement.

(5) Mainline denominations have been losing members for decades, while conservative denominations have been growing.

(6) At the present rates of change, Islam may well become the dominant religion in the world by 2050.

(7) At the present rate of change, most people will identify themselves as non-religious or non-Christian by the year 2035.

(8) The number of "un-churched" people—individuals who have not attended church in recent months—has increased rapidly.

(9) The number of agnostics, atheists, and secularists is growing.

(10)   Interest in new religious movements (e.g., New Age, Neo-paganism) is growing rapidly, with Wiccans doubling in numbers about every 30 months.

(11)   The influence of the central, program-based congregation is diminishing, as more cell churches are being created.[30]

The above sampling, while not exhaustive, offers a portrait of the rapidly changing religious landscape. The plethora of trends impacting spirituality can be reduced to four mega-trends. These mega-trends represent shifts in perception regarding particular aspects of faith.[31]

Ecumenical to Interfaith

As noted above, American religious expression has been historically and primarily Judeo-Christian. A high percentage of persons lived their entire lives within a particular faith tradition. However, a shift toward diversity, tolerance and the acceptance of other faith traditions is now noticeable. Although ecumenical cooperation among faith traditions is present, specifically within the Judeo-Christian context, there is also a growing interest and participation in interfaith cooperation. Perhaps nowhere is this more evident than with the recent integration of Islam into America's public religious observance. Since September 11, 2001, the date of the terrorist attacks on the World Trade Center in New York City, an intentional effort has been made within many sectors to integrate Islam into America's religious landscape. Since Judaism, Christianity and Islam view the Old Testament as a sacred text, for many the inclusion of Islam into the public religious life of the nation is the natural course of action.

Interfaith cooperation will no doubt continue to characterize contemporary religious life, especially in the public arena. The current tendency toward political correctness and the rejection of all things intolerant will almost certainly mandate a continuation of this mega-trend.

Prophetic to Political

From its inception, America was established on the premise of a Judeo-Christian worldview, and society at large functioned within those boundaries. Social concerns from both the religious and secular sectors were viewed and engaged within this worldview. However, as American society became increasingly diverse, ecclesiastical groups, para-church ministries and denominations began to address social concerns through political means. This approach became clearly visible in the 1960's, as various denominational bodies established public resolutions regarding the issue of civil rights.

Since the early 1980's, numerous entities have been established to impact and influence American culture through the political process. Organizations such as the Moral Majority, Focus on the Family, American Family Association, American Centre for Law and Justice, and the Christian Coalition have sought to influence social concerns and policy based on a Judeo-Christian worldview. Public positions from these organizations and numerous ecclesiastical and denominational groups on issues such as abortion, euthanasia, capital punishment, stem-cell research and AIDS have been established. The implementation of faith-based initiatives by former U.S. President George W. Bush is perhaps an outgrowth of this trend from prophetic to political. Social concerns, no longer the agenda of board meetings or seasonal sermons, have become the business of the religious landscape. This trend will no doubt continue to influence contemporary religious life.

Word to Spirit

Our religious orientation has historically been rooted in the Word, based on a collection of beliefs and doctrines directly drawn from Scripture. Preaching most often focuses on meaning and explanation, focusing on matters of biblical interpretation in order to provide a foundation for offering application. However, a shift is occurring toward a religious perspective oriented to the Spirit. Here, the emphasis is experiential and subjective. The preaching style tends to be narrative rather than explanatory; and, while belief and doctrinal concerns are rooted in Scripture, they may draw from other sources as well.

Recent research reveals that 72% of adults view their spiritual orientation as *personal and individual,* rather than through *organized religion and church doctrine.*[32] The continuation of this trend will present numerous methodological challenges for the transitioning religious landscape.

Mission to Worship

While almost every norm of the Christian faith experienced a shift in methods of doing ministry, worship in many mainline denominations remained entrenched in a 1950's model. The primary emphasis for many of these churches was mission. In recent years, however, recognizing that genuine worship is a predecessor of mission, many of these faith traditions have rediscovered the wonder of worship. Nearly one-third of liberal Protestant churches have experienced significant change in their style of worship during the previous five years.[33] Because of this the term "worship wars" has been coined, with the transition in worship style producing conflict in many congregations. Yet, this trend continues to make a huge impact on the religious scene. Many churches that once opposed the use of electric guitars and drums have now incorporated them into their mode of worship. Contemporary music styles, praise and worship bands, and high-energy worship dominate today's religious scene.

Given the influx of these trends, where will they take the church? Where will it end? It is impossible to know for sure, however, several possibilities exist:

(1)   Increasing diversity across religious groups

(2)   Increasing diversity within religious groups

(3)   Increasing the subjective and spiritual aspects of religious expression

(4)   Increasing the primary business of worshiping God[34]

Trends in Contemporary Religious Beliefs and Behavior

Not only are there trends that can be derived from empirical research regarding the current religious landscape at large, there are also trends that define the religious beliefs and behavior of Christians. The Barna Group recently conducted an extensive survey of religion in contemporary society, documenting the research data in a publication entitled, *The State of the Church: 2006*. The data reveals cause for both concern and hope for the future of religious expression and faith. The following sampling of religious beliefs and behavior will be briefly discussed.

Religious Beliefs

Since the beginning of the Republic, the vast majority of Americans have considered themselves Christian. This group currently makes up approximately 84% of the population, varying by region, ethnicity, age, gender and political preference. Protestants comprise roughly 57% of this adult public, with Catholics comprising some 24%. Notice the level of commitment to the Christian faith among professing believers: 54% considered themselves absolutely committed, 37% were moderately committed, 6% were not too committed, and 2% were not committed at all. A large group, 71%, viewed God as the all-knowing, all-powerful, perfect creator of the universe who rules the world today. Of those who believed the Bible to be totally accurate in all the principles it teaches, 48% agreed strongly, 20% agreed somewhat, 15% disagreed somewhat, 13% strongly disagreed, and 4% didn't know. Of those who believed they had a personal responsibility to share their faith, 39% strongly agreed with another 16% who agreed somewhat.[35]

The question was posed as to whether the participant's religious faith was very important in his/her life. 69% agreed strongly that it was, 16% agreed somewhat, and approximately 15% disagreed or didn't know. Another belief statement posed to the participants was, "When He lived on earth, Jesus Christ was human and committed sins like other people." Approximately 23% agreed strongly, 19% agreed somewhat, and 52% disagreed. Regarding the statement that belonging to a community of faith was necessary for spiritual completion and maturity, only 34% agreed, while 63% disagreed. Regarding the question of those who had made a personal commitment to Jesus Christ, 45% responded in the affirmative. This brief sampling of contemporary beliefs in the contemporary religious community is only a microcosm of a much broader belief system. However, it does offer a basic understanding of current belief trends.

Religious Behavior

Religious behavior is not always consistent with prevailing belief patterns. Although 68% believed the Bible to be accurate in all its principles, only 47% had read from the Bible in the seven days prior to the survey. While 84% of the participants claimed to be Christian, only 47% had attended a church service in the week prior to the survey. One of the most consistent behavioral patterns involved praying to God, with 84% of the participants responding in the affirmative. When asked if they had shared their religious beliefs with others during the preceding twelve months, 60% responded in the affirmative.

Other patterns of behavior demonstrated much lower percentages. Regarding the tithe, the giving of 10% or more of one's annual income, only 5% of adult Christians (8% of evangelicals) did so the year prior to the survey. Only 27% of the participants had volunteered time to help the church. Approximately 23% had met with other believers for the purpose of Bible study, small group ministry, prayer or Christian fellowship.

Behavioral patterns between Christians and non-Christians were alarmingly similar. Of the twenty-five specific lifestyle practices noted in the survey, ranging from giving to a charity, buying a lottery ticket, or watching an R-rated movie, the difference between Christian and non-Christian behavior was minuscule.[36] At the critical level, the implication is that Christians often behave no differently than anyone else. This fact alone presents numerous challenges for engaging the culture with the life-changing message of the gospel of Jesus Christ. It further validates the purpose of this book.

Postmodernism
The Context of the Contemporary Church

According to I Chronicles 12:32, the men of Issachar *understood the times and knew what Israel should do*. The ability to understand the times in which they lived allowed the men of Issachar to make wise decisions regarding Israel's current and future objectives. Understanding the context of the church inevitably includes an understanding of the current context within which the church resides. Postmodernism, with its myriad nuances, is that context.

Historically, Western culture has been categorized into three broad eras of time: pre-modernism, modernism and postmodernism. Each is characterized by unique philosophical, sociological and religious descriptors. Recognition of the primary elements of each era and the way each transitions to the next allows one to understand the contemporary context of postmodernism.

Pre-modernism

The pre-modern period covers human history from creation to approximately 1500 A.D., encompassing both the ancient and medieval periods. Pre-modern cultures were characterized by a belief that the natural world did not comprise the entire essence of reality. In religious terms, lines of demarcation were drawn regarding the natural and the supernatural, with the corresponding belief in God or gods. For the most part, these cultures had limited religious or cultural diversity and minimal social change.

For Western culture, the grand example of pre-modern existence was the rise of Christianity.[37] This period was distinguished by the worldview that an omnipotent God had created the entire universe and the human race and had a plan that he was ordaining.[38] United by a particular faith tradition one that stipulated codes of conduct and societal norms Christians considered other religious faiths to be marginal. While non-Christian religions did indeed exist, Christianity was a key factor in the cultural stability that existed during this period.

The Renaissance (1350-1600) marked the beginning of a shift from medieval norms to a new interest in knowledge, and in particular, the heritage of ancient Greek civilization.[39] Containing both Christian and non-Christian elements, Renaissance proponents challenged established theological and cultural opinions and explored pre-Christian Greek thought for neglected insights.[40]

As change occurred in the disciplines of art, academia and philosophy, Christianity itself began to experience a metamorphosis. The period 1300-1500 gave rise to numerous attempts at reforming Roman Catholicism, culminating in the reform efforts of a Catholic monk named Martin Luther (1483-1546). Luther's efforts ignited the Protestant Reformation, which challenged the religious monopoly held by the Roman Catholic Church. These events facilitated the transition from pre-modernism to modernism.

Modernism

The Renaissance, along with the Reformation, created the cultural, religious and social climate, which gave birth to the period known as the Enlightenment, or the Age of Reason. Encompassing the 17th and 18th centuries, the Enlightenment initiated the transition from the pre-modern to modern era. Perceptions long held by Christians regarding theology, anthropology, sociology, philosophy, science and the world at large began to change. The questioning of almost every societal norm energized the skepticism which became the nucleus of the Enlightenment, the exaltation of human reason above all else.

Personalities such as Rene Descartes (1596-1650), John Locke (1632-1704), David Hume (1711-1776) and Immanuel Kant (1724-1804) led the thrust toward modernity. These proponents sought all-inclusive explanations of events and of reality but believed this could be done without recourse to anything supernatural.[41] Several motifs helped set in motion modernity's formation. First, *foundationalism* postulated the existence of beliefs and experiences upon which systems of belief could be established. Second, *structuralism* taught that cultures and societies develop texts to define the meaning of life in general, and that those texts, by means of the interpretive method of reason, could be collectively understood. Third *meta-narrative*, the compilation of stories within a text, could help define human existence by providing a logical sequence of events regarding the main issues of life.

Modernism was not relegated merely to the philosophical or scientific but also covered a broad spectrum of disciplines. Every facet of life was influenced by some aspect of modernism. Modernism was not merely a period of temporal duration but was also a period committed to the advancement of the Enlightenment worldview.[42] This brief synopsis of both the pre-modern and modern periods facilitates a better understanding of the development and tenets of postmodernism. It also helps underscore many of the trends seen within the contemporary context.

Postmodernism

Science, reason and progress were regarded by proponents of modernism as humankind's sources for emancipation from the shackles of pre-modernity. Utopian expectations produced by the Enlightenment, however, failed to materialize. Therefore, by the 20th century the optimism that characterized modernity began to fragment. Digressing social, economic and moral conditions resulted in a cynicism toward the utopian expectations associated with modernism. Reaction to the prevailing state of affairs became a catalyst for the transition from modernism to postmodernism. Proponents of postmodernism abandoned long-held positions established by the scientific method of the Enlightenment.

Disillusionment with modernism was only one factor contributing to the emergence of postmodernism. The influence of philosophy was integral to the process. The philosophical roots of postmodernism began to materialize in the ideas proposed by Friedrich Nietzsche (1844-1900). Deviating from modernity's established notion that language conveyed truth, Nietzsche proposed that individual interpretation of language was instrumental to understanding human existence. Nietzsche sought to validate his philosophical leanings by asserting the death of God hypothesis.

Several philosophical contributions facilitated the transition from modernism to postmodernism.[43] First, egocentrism, the preoccupation with self rather than God, came to be the philosophical reference point. As a result selfism became one of postmodernity's many religions. Second, existentialism followed egocentricism. Concepts such as intrinsic value, universal morality and a legitimate meta-narrative are deemed to be only mythical. Third, nihilism, the belief that absolute truth is impossible to ascertain, inevitably followed egocentricism and existentialism. Nihilism asserts that human existence has no clear explanation or purpose, ultimately producing a mindset that resists moral accountability and personal responsibility. Consequently, postmodernism can be characterized as a complete denunciation and departure from the Enlightenment worldview. The result is a worldview that elevates the individual to the status of becoming one's own god.

The above tenets—products of postmodernism—communicate the environment of the 21st century church. Just as the sons of Issachar understood the times of ancient Israel, the social, moral and economic context in which they lived, an understanding of contemporary times will facilitate effective Christian living.

The Characteristics of Postmodernism

Contemporary culture is not the first to encounter the influence of postmodern characteristics, for both the Old and New Testaments provide parallels. The early period of Israel's assimilation into the demography of Canaan is recorded in the Old Testament book of Judges. In Judges 17:1—21:25 a specific period of religious, civil and moral disorder is depicted. The chronic refrain of this period is found in Judges 21:25 (NASB), *In those days there was no king in Israel; every man did what was right in his own eyes.* An assessment of this period reveals several characteristics that parallel postmodernism: 1) rejection of divine authority; 2) religious relativism; 3) moral instability; 4) social and political fragmentation; and 5) pragmatism.

The New Testament book of Acts (17:16-34) depicts the narrative of Paul's ministry in the city of Athens, Greece. Paul discovered the extreme religious and philosophical pluralism as well as the moral debauchery that dominated the city. Athens was an intellectual and cultural think tank, where, according to Acts 17:21 (NASB), participants would *spend their time in nothing other than telling or hearing something new.* The Athenian context also reveals characteristics that parallel postmodernism: 1)pluralism; 2) relativism; and 3) rejection of absolute truth.

A brief overview of postmodernism, observed within the framework of its social and philosophical antecedents, is foundational for understanding the contemporary context of the church. Christianity at large has been profoundly influenced by the secular world in which it resides. Although this book does not attempt to offer an exhaustive treatment, an overview of certain significant tenets of postmodernism is offered. The transition to postmodernism in American culture occurred during the 1960's and 1970's. These tumultuous decades produced a generation that rejected cultural norms, ultimately affecting almost every segment of society. While not a comprehensive list, the following characteristics help define postmodernism.

Privatized Faith

Religious belief and practice, once hallmarks of communities at large, become expressions of the individual in postmodernism. While the number of Americans who view themselves as Christians is in the eightieth percentile (84%), only half (47%) consistently attends church or participates in organized religion. Terms and phrases such as *post-church*, *churchless* and *church for those who don't do church* have been coined to describe postmodernism's tendency to reject organized religion, opting instead for the private expression of faith. Because of this, the church has become largely irrelevant to many.

The privatization of faith has led to a sort of spiritual individualism where self reigns supreme. In this context no particular faith is more authoritative or relevant than another. The observance of religion has not been eradicated from the public arena; rather, it has been privatized within the lives of individual believers. The privatization of faith lends itself to religious pluralism.

Pluralized Belief

Perhaps the most defining tenet of postmodernism is its rejection of the notion that truth can be known in absolute terms. In pre-modernism, the concept of truth was the culmination of faith in God or gods. Modernism lifted up the scientific method as the valid source of truth. In postmodernism, however, truth is contextually subjective. The individual (or group) sets his or her (its) own standard of what is acceptable and what isn't. The Reformation concept of *sola scriptura*, in postmodernism is replaced with tolerance. The expectation is to be tolerant of any and all belief systems.

Within the defining terms of this characteristic, all belief systems are viewed as valid expressions of faith. The postmodern worldview embraces with the same level legitimacy all belief systems, such as Christianity, Islam, Judaism, Wicca, Hinduism, and even those who have no belief system at all. Since individual or group dynamics have replaced established truth patterns, everyone is right, and no one is wrong.

Marginalized Religion

The exclusion of religious faith from the public arena, which is the inevitable outcome of privatized faith and pluralized belief, eventually leads to the demise of religious observance and a resultant secularism. Non-sectarian perceptions of morality are also discarded in favor of neutrality in such matters. At this point in the transition almost every societal norm is affected. Art, education, politics, social ideas, are all expunged of religious influence. Even among those sympathetic to maintaining some semblance of religious influence, fear of litigation is often a mitigating factor in their refusal to do so.

In the marginalization of religion, current contextual entities often play the role of devil's advocate.[44] For example, the media often delights in portraying the religious—especially evangelical Christians—as bigoted, mean-spirited and hateful. When the portrayal is sympathetic at all, it is intentionally biased. While tolerance is touted as the expected norm, it is not equally distributed to all involved. Evangelical Christians in particular are expected to be tolerant of all others yet are often not extended the same level of tolerance.

Relativized Values

The privatization of faith leads to pluralism of belief, both of which lead to the marginalization of religion in the public sector. When religion is no longer allowed to influence culture, the basis for absolute values is destroyed. This leads to the gradual implementation of relativized values, based not upon religious principles but upon the pragmatic philosophy of "Does it work?" Once such criteria are established as the guiding principles for values formation, everything becomes relative. This line of reasoning leads to living for the moment with nothing more than a loose set of ideals—ideals that are often in conflict with one another and are frequently abandoned if the situation warrants.[45]

As values become increasingly relative, individual or group dynamics reign supreme. Accepted norms from prior generations or cultures are no longer viewed with the same vigor. Since adaptation to newer norms is never immediate, the process of values clarification is necessary. This alienates religious influence from the affairs of life, leading those involved further from the moorings of absolute truth.

Opportunities of Postmodernism

While postmodernism does indeed present many challenges for the church, it also offers several opportunities.[46]

Proclamation of the Gospel

Postmodernism, first, presents an opportunity for the proclamation of the Christian gospel. Modernity's claim that reason and the scientific method are the criteria for discovering truth is rejected by the postmodernist. Instead, alternative sources for discovering and knowing truth are given consideration. In the postmodern context, revealed truth or truths again become an option. Presented as an alternative source to the claims of modernity, the Christian gospel can be given credence, which inevitably allows for its proclamation. This mandates an adequate response by the church regarding the current abundance of truth claims.

Commitment to Pluralism

Postmodernism's commitment to pluralism offers a second opportunity for the church. Pluralism with its myriad paths to enlightenment projects a certain animosity toward the organized Christian faith. Tolerance of each and every belief system, often to the exclusion of Christianity, is expected. Although postmodernism is often unsympathetic toward Christians, it is often sympathetic to Jesus. If, as pluralism suggests, all religious systems are valid paths to enlightenment, then Christianity warrants equal consideration. Anything less violates the postmodern allegiance to tolerance. Therefore, an opportunity exists for Christians to assist in expanding the Kingdom of God on earth.

Quest for Spirituality

Inherent within postmodernism is a quest for spirituality. This presents a third opportunity for the American church. The contemporary affinity for spirituality has produced a mixed bag—traditional and experimental, mainstream and fringe, Christ-centered and syncretistic.[47] This climate of ambiguity, produced by postmodernism's inability to satisfy the spiritual appetite of the soul, offers an opportunity to present Jesus Christ as the only legitimate source of spirituality.

Conclusion

This chapter has explored the context of the church in the first decade of the 21st century. For better or worse, it is here the church currently resides. The numerous challenges of postmodernism profoundly influence contemporary Christianity. Because this is true, contemporary believers must do what generations of Christians have done—examine once again the biblical, theological and ethical foundations for Christian living. This pursuit must not be understood as an attempt to secure salvation by works. On the contrary, it is an attempt to understand the fundamental importance of a life altered and changed by the power of Christ. It is an effort to find that place where life and faith meet, where belief and behavior merge, and where, through the power of the Holy Spirit, one is enabled to live the victorious life of faith. It is here that one is able to impact one's context and culture with the gospel of Jesus Christ.

PART TWO

EXAMINING THE FOUNDATIONS

Chapter Three

Biblical Foundations for the Christian Life

All guidelines for Christian behavior must find their origin in Scripture. Anything less is extra-biblical. Lifestyle requirements and behavioral boundaries not found in Scripture often form the basis for legalism and cults. Because this is true, it is imperative that a biblical foundation for Christian living be established. In this chapter a biblical foundation is offered regarding the significance of Christian life and behavior. Two components are considered: 1) a synopsis of biblical ethics; and 2) several key passages that establish the correlation between life and faith.

A Synopsis of Biblical Ethics

Central to the theme of this book is the correlation between belief and behavior. Early in the covenant relationship God's mandate to Israel is set forth. *I am the LORD who brought you up out of Egypt to be your God; therefore be holy, because I am holy* (Leviticus 11:45). Here, God presents a premise for belief by telling his people: *I am the LORD who brought you up out of Egypt to be your God*. The Israelites are to believe this truth, and respond accordingly by pursuing holiness (*be holy*) in their behavior and manner of life. This aspect of biblical ethics is a consistent theme throughout both the Old and New Testaments.

Old Testament Ethical Foundations

An emphasis on ethical issues (belief and behavior) is visible early in human history, in terms of both a relationship with God and interpersonal human relationships. Ethical principles are found within each genre of Old Testament literature. This is first observed in the creation ordinances, where an emphasis is placed on the procreation of offspring, replenishing and subduing the earth, dominion over created things, labor, the Sabbath and marriage.[48]

As early as the creation narrative, the God of the Bible establishes a particular ethical standard by which His creation is to be accountable. This ethic is not a mere adherence to a legalistic code of conduct. It is a direct reflection of the covenant relationship with the God of the Bible.[49]

> A fundamental continuity prevails between Old and New Testament teaching. Hence, an understanding of Hebrew ethics is essential to an adequate knowledge of the ethics of Jesus and the New Testament as a whole. Christian ethics, therefore, requires an analysis of the characteristics and content of the main streams of morality in the Old Covenant.[50]

In order to gain a better understanding of ethics in the Old Testament, the following categories are briefly examined: 1) ethics in the Decalogue; 2) ethics in the wisdom literature; and 3) ethics in the prophetic literature.

Ethics in the Decalogue

The Old Testament refers to the Decalogue, perhaps better known as the Ten Commandments, as *ten words* (Deuteronomy 4:13; 10:4), or *the words of the covenant* (Exodus 34:28). The Decalogue is central to the Old Testament narrative. Presented as a list of succinct ethical statements, the Decalogue is designed to offer boundaries for the lifestyle and behavioral practices of God's people. Each of the covenantal statements contains guidelines for practical living:

(1)   You shall have no other gods before me.

(2)   You shall not make for yourself an idol in the form of anything.

(3)   You shall not misuse the name of the LORD your God.

(4)   Remember the Sabbath day by keeping it holy.

(5)   Honor your father and your mother.

(6)   You shall not murder.

(7)   You shall not commit adultery.

(8)   You shall not steal.

(9)   You shall not give false testimony against your neighbor.

(10)   You shall not covet (Exodus 20:3-17).

Within these *ten words*, a system of ethical accountability is set forth and further expanded throughout the Pentateuch in terms of specific behavioral practices. However, the Decalogue is more than a mere collection of customs and habits.[51] These moral injunctions are commands of God, constituting universal and eternal values that are integral for the fulfillment of individual and societal morality. This is of primary importance. Successful incorporation of such injunctions mandates the belief that God requires obedience to these commands. The essence of the covenant relationship is fundamental to the appropriation of the Decalogue's ethical principles.

Ethics in the Wisdom Literature

Within the wisdom literature (Job, Psalms, Proverbs, Ecclesiastes and the Song of Songs) there is a definite ethical focus that is primarily practical in emphasis. Within this genre of literature the relationship between belief and behavior is clearly visible. For example, consider the emphasis of each book as it highlights a particular aspect of ethical behavior in response to God's covenant relationship with His people:

(1)   Job: Loyalty to God in the midst of suffering

(2)   Psalms: A great and good God in a godless world

(3)   Proverbs: Practical morality in all walks of life

(4)   Ecclesiastes: Fear God and keep his commandments

(5)   Song of Songs: The faithfulness of true love

The wisdom literature teaches individuals the application of ethical principles in the light of experience.[52] The writers seek to convey the essence of ethics in such a way as to empower the individual to successfully live out one's moral obligations within society at large. For the wisdom writers, the aspect of community is fundamental to biblical ethics. While a relationship with God is inherent, it is within the context of community that ethical behavior finds its most valuable framework.

Ethics in the Prophetic Literature

The prophets of Israel, both writing and non-writing, are individuals who function as agents of change. They serve as preachers of personal righteousness, advocates for the rights of humankind and persons of hope in a world often lacking such principles.[53] They preach against the sins of the people, which most often involve a violation of God's covenant with them and their mistreatment of those within the covenant community.[54] The following examples highlight the ethical focus of the prophetic literature:

(1)   Amos cries for justice among the people of God.

(2)   Hosea reveals God's love toward his wayward people.

(3)   Micah exposes the sins of Jerusalem and cities in general.

(3)   Ezekiel discloses the specific sins of Israel's leadership.

(5)   Jeremiah focuses on Israel's personal responsibility to God.

The ethics of the prophets originate from their theology, in that right behavior depends on knowing God and sharing his concerns in the life of the community.[55] Operating from this premise the objectives of the prophets are: 1) to reveal to their audience the lack of righteousness; 2) to warn of the dangers of continuing to practice unrighteousness; and 3) to emphasize the rewards of pursuing righteousness. From a prophetic perspective, righteousness is visible primarily in one's manner of life and moral conduct.

The theme of biblical ethics is clearly visible in each of the above Old Testament categories. Obedience to God's will as the basis for character and conduct is the guiding principle of Old Testament ethics.[56]

New Testament Ethical Foundations

Building on Old Testament ethical foundations, ethical emphases in the New Testament focus on the covenant relationship between God and humankind based on the ministry of Jesus Christ. The ethical emphasis at this point involves primarily the Christian community. Although outsiders may indeed admire certain aspects of New Testament moral teaching, only those who participate in the faith life of the believing community can fully appreciate its ethic.[57] Participation in the believing community is understood as the New Covenant relationship that is entered by way of repentance.

The following New Testament categories are briefly examined: 1) ethics in the life and ministry of Jesus; 2) ethics in the Pauline; and 3) ethics in the non-Pauline literature.

Ethics in the Life and Ministry of Jesus

Central to a New Testament ethic is the life and ministry of Jesus. Of Jesus, *all the prophets testify* (Acts 10:43). In Jesus, the Law is fulfilled (Matthew 5:17). Through Jesus, the moral teachings of the Old Testament find completion. The ethics of Jesus embody the standard of righteousness that a holy God requires from his people.[58] The ethical teachings of Jesus are essentially connected to obedience. By means of obedience, motivation is found for dedicating one's entire life to God. The result of this relationship is the intentional conforming of all conduct to the standard of Jesus' righteousness.[59]

While not a complete statement of Jesus' ethics, Matthew 5-7 sets forth the basis of his moral teachings. In the Sermon on the Mount, Jesus places a new emphasis upon the inseparable relationship between theology and ethics (belief and behavior).[60] He summarizes the content of the sermon as: 1) Christian character (Matthew 5:3-12); 2) Christian corollary (Matthew 5:13-16); and 3) Christian conduct (Matthew 5:17-7:12). In the Sermon on the Mount, Jesus introduces the principles that will characterize living within the kingdom he came to initiate, the Kingdom of God.

Perhaps the most succinct statement of Jesus' ethics is found in Matthew 22:37-39, *Love the Lord your God with all your heart and with all your soul and with all your mind. This is the first and greatest commandment. And the second is like it: Love your neighbor as yourself.* Righteousness finds its fullest expression in the principle of love, which is central to the entire body of Jesus' moral teachings. The ethics of Jesus is based upon the close relationship between a love for God and a love for one's neighbor and in the absolute priority of love above all other virtues.[61]

Ethics in the Pauline Literature

It does not seem to be Paul's objective to set forth a systematic presentation of Christian ethics. Nor does Paul offer a comprehensive summary of duties and responsibilities. Rather, Pauline ethics finds its origin in the ethics of Jesus. Although Paul expands on many of the moral principles presented by Jesus, he never opposes them, nor does he introduce something different. According to Paul, Christian believers are to live *according to Christ* (Colossians 2:8, NASB). Inauguration into a biblically ethical life comes from a relationship with Christ. The result of this relationship is that *if anyone is in Christ, he is a new creation; the old has gone, the new has come* (II Corinthians 5:17). In this passage, Paul instructs those who are in Christ to live upright lives, because the new life demands moral conduct.[62]

Paul reveals the impossibility of attaining the ethical teachings of Jesus merely by human effort. Attainment of such is possible only through the enablement of the Holy Spirit residing within the believer (Romans 3:20; 6:12-14; 8:3-4). Through the Holy Spirit the believer is *being transformed into his* [Jesus'] *likeness* (II Corinthians 3:18). This process allows the believer to emulate Jesus in terms of inner ethical convictions.[63]

In Pauline ethics, one aspect of the new life is found in the immediate circle of the family. Paul's ethical instructions regarding marriage, divorce, remarriage, parenting, and interpersonal issues within the home, all emphasize a well-ordered home life. Positive ethical behavior within the context of the family is critical, for it is here in the primary unit of human community, that Christian love finds its basic expression.

Ethics in the Non-Pauline Literature

Apart from the Gospels and Pauline letters, the remaining New Testament literature is also concerned with ethical matters. This literature highlights the issue of Christian conduct, both personal and social.[64] It places emphasis on the ethics of Jesus as the ultimate model for Christian belief and behavior. For example,

(1)   The writer of Hebrews warns of *disobedience* (Hebrews 2:2), while instructing the reader to focus *on Jesus, the author and perfecter of our faith* (Hebrews 12:2).

(2)   James offers very practical guidelines for Christian behavior, based on the premise that his readers are *believers in our glorious Lord Jesus Christ* (James 2:1).

(3)   Peter emphasizes the necessity of *doing good* (I Peter 2:15, 20; 3:17) and ethical behavior that arises from *obedience to Jesus Christ* (I Peter 1:2).

(4)   John accentuates the ethics of Jesus by noting that it is impossible to *have fellowship with him yet walk in the darkness* (I John 1:6).

(5) Jude asserts that because believers are *kept by Jesus Christ* (Jude 1), they are not to change God's grace into a *license for immorality* (Jude 4).

In general, ethics in the non-Pauline literature is based on human conduct being subject to a standard of unconditional value, namely, the righteousness of God.[65] This standard is personified in the ethics of Jesus.

Indeed, the theme of biblical ethics is found throughout both the Old and New Testaments. Central to God's revelation to his people is the component of the covenant relationship, where belief and behavior are intentionally connected, with the latter being the end result of the former.

Three Key Passages Relating to Biblical Ethics

In the following key passages, the essence of biblical ethics—the relationship between belief and behavior—is observed as the model for Christian living. This section does not offer an exhaustive list of passages, but it serves to highlight the importance of biblical ethics to the Christian life.

Romans 12:1-2

Paul's letter to the Romans highlights the theme of salvation, which is understood in terms of the righteousness of God. Central to this theme is the issue of biblical ethics. It is evident that Paul does not set forth his theological teaching merely for informational purposes, but to give a foundation for transformed conduct. Biblical doctrine is never taught simply to be known, but primarily that it may be translated into practice.[66] This is clear in the Romans 12:1-2 passage, where, after eleven chapters of a theological and doctrinal nature, Paul offers the following practical instruction,

> *Therefore, I urge you, brothers, in view of God's mercy, to offer your bodies as living sacrifices, holy and pleasing to God—this is your spiritual act of worship. Do not conform any longer to the pattern of this world, but be transformed*

> *by the renewing of your mind. Then you will be able to test and approve what God's will is—his good, pleasing and perfect will.*

This passage serves as an introductory prelude to the discussion of specific ethical duties, setting forth the fundamental obligations that must be met in order to face the challenge of living in the world as a believer.[67] Paul's admonitions are specific: 1) offer your bodies as living sacrifices; 2) live holy lives pleasing to God; 3) live no longer like the world; and 4) be transformed into the image of Christ.

Galatians 5:19-24

In his treatise on Christian liberty, Paul sets forth the doctrinal tenet of justification by faith. Key to this doctrine is the fundamental teaching of grace—that salvation is obtained by God's grace through faith in Jesus Christ. This results in a new and transformed way of living. While the letter to the Galatians does indeed focus on salvation by faith, this new and transformed way of living is characterized by the practical demands of Christian living.[68] In the main, Christian liberty does not invalidate biblical ethics. Galatians 5:19-24 places a line of demarcation between sinful and spiritual living in the following terms,

> *The acts of the sinful nature are obvious: sexual immorality, impurity and debauchery; idolatry and witchcraft; hatred, discord, jealousy, fits of rage, selfish ambition, dissensions, factions and envy; drunkenness, orgies, and the like. I warn you, as I did before, that those who live like this will not inherit the kingdom of God. But the fruit of the Spirit is love, joy, peace, patience, kindness, goodness, faithfulness, gentleness and self-control. Against such things there is no law. Those who belong to Christ Jesus have crucified the sinful nature with its passions and desires.*

The essence of biblical ethics is again evident in that the Galatian believers, and ultimately believers in every age, are assured that by way of the New Covenant relationship, Christ provides the enablement to crucify the sinful nature with its passions and desires.

Colossians 3:5-10

Paul's theological emphasis in the letter to the Colossian believers is the supremacy and sufficiency of Jesus Christ. As in the previous two passages, here, too, the relationship between belief and behavior is understood. In Colossians 3:5-10 Paul instructs his audience to,

> *Put to death, therefore, whatever belongs to your earthly nature: sexual immorality, impurity, lust, evil desires and greed, which is idolatry. Because of these, the wrath of God is coming. You used to walk in these ways, in the life you once lived. But now you must rid yourselves of all such things as these: anger, rage, malice, slander, and filthy language from your lips. Do not lie to each other, since you have taken off your old self with its practices and have put on the new self, which is being renewed in knowledge in the image of its Creator.*

By candidly naming sinful practices, Paul sets a clear standard for the church in that such behavior is incompatible with the transformed life.[69] The connection between theology and ethics is paramount in this passage as Paul firmly asserts, *you have taken off your old self with its practices and have put on the new self* [with its practices] (Colossians 3:9b-10a).

The emphasis on biblical ethics is inherent in each of the three key passages. By way of the New Covenant a new and transformed life is established, characterized by the ethics of Jesus. Herein lie the foundations for all matters of Christian living, behavior, and moral conduct.

CHAPTER FOUR

A Theological Basis for Christian Ethics

Christian ethics is fundamentally about living the Christian life. Modern culture, American culture in particular, is experiencing a moral crisis of dramatic proportion. Standards of behavior once held sacred are no longer viewed as such. Note the following evidences of this current moral crisis:

(1)   Escalating violence

(2)   Corruption in leadership

(3)   Gaps in lifestyle

(4)   Alcohol and drug use and abuse

(5)   Poverty

(6)   Racism

(7)   Family breakdown

(8)   Consumerism and materialism[70]

The moral crisis affects not only secular society but also Christ's Church. Because this is true, a biblically informed Christian ethic is of paramount importance to effectively engage the present generation.

Throughout the Bible, in both the Old and New Testaments, the people of God are differentiated from all others. While primarily a matter of the heart, this difference is most evident in the specific lifestyle and behavior of God's people. Ethics involves standards of behavior that dictate how one should conduct oneself in a given situation. The word *ethics* is derived from the Greek term *ethos* (ἔθος), which has reference to custom, usage, manner of life, or pattern of conduct.[71] Although ethics resides within the discipline of systematic theology, it is important to correctly distinguish between the two. Theology is concerned primarily with how persons should think, while ethics is concerned with how persons should live.[72] In this regard, Christian ethics may be defined as dedicating one's whole life to God daily and conforming all conduct to the standard of his righteousness.[73] For this reason Christian ethics is not merely a set of beliefs or application of those beliefs but also the foundation upon which those beliefs are determined. From this foundational premise, spiritual growth is inevitable. Spiritual growth is the progressive increase or development in certain areas of one's spiritual life and its experience.[74] This view is validated in Paul's letter to the Ephesians (4:11-16), where believers are depicted as becoming mature and growing up in Christ.

Christian ethics has to do with a particular quality of holiness expected of the people of God—a lifestyle of sanctification and purity. The basis of this expectation resides in the covenant relationship between Christ and the believer—the new covenant wrought and established by Christ.[75] Biblical support for this position is found in Romans 12:1, where Paul writes, *I urge you, brothers, in view of God's mercy, to offer your bodies as living sacrifices, holy and pleasing to God—this is your spiritual act of worship.* The covenantal relationship calls for a new mind, a new heart, a new spirit, and thus, a new way of living.[76]

The Christian lifestyle is not given in a neatly wrapped package at one's profession of faith. It is a lifestyle that progresses as one's relationship with Christ develops and matures. This relationship sets forth specific criteria for affecting one's behavior and manner of life. Again, this is incumbent on the Christian by virtue of one's relationship with Jesus

Christ. In this regard, biblical principles of conduct are established as a model for living the Christian life. It is here that theology relates to practical living rather than merely to belief alone.

In general terms, ethical inquiry is a journey into one's moral nature for the purpose of discovering areas of personal responsibility and how to fulfill them. The following themes are examined in this chapter: 1) contemporary ethical systems; 2) Christian ethics; 3) problems in Christian ethics; and 4) Christian ethics as an adequate ethical system.

Contemporary Ethical Systems

The study of ethics is important for several reasons. First, Western culture has relinquished any absolute framework for thinking about ethical standards. Second, the "slippery slope" nature of so many ethical questions needs to be addressed. Third, Christians need to understand the integrated nature of ethical issues. Fourth, many Christians know where they stand on certain ethical issues, but they do not know how to defend their position.[77] Numerous ethical systems set forth criteria for the understanding and determination of truth, each with its own advocates, adherents and opponents. A brief evaluation of the following ethical systems is offered.

Cultural Relativism

Cultural relativism holds at its core the belief that ethics is defined by culture. Assertions of what is right and wrong and what make them such become the interpretation of the majority within a given culture. While cultures may indeed learn from each other, no particular culture is the sole arbiter of truth. Inherent within this ethical system are at least two fundamental variables: 1) because truth is perceived as relative, there are no absolutes; and 2) since cultures evolve regarding their moral positions, truth is in a permanent state of transition.

The following observations reveal the inadequacy of cultural relativism to effectively address the current moral climate of society at large.

(1)   It is not enough to say that morals originate in the world and are constantly evolving. Cultural relativism fails to answer how values originate from nothing.

(2)   Cultural relativism seems to hold as a cardinal truth that values change. But, if the truth that values change is itself unchanging, this theory claims as an unchanging truth that all values change and progress. Thus, the position contradicts itself.

(3)   If there are no absolute values that exist trans-culturally or externally to the group, how are different cultures to get along when values collide? How are they to handle such conflicts?

(4)   Where does a group or culture get its authority? Why can't individuals assume that authority?

(5)   Most of our heroes and heroines have been those who courageously went against culture and justified their actions by appealing to a higher standard. According to cultural relativism, such people are always morally wrong.

(6)   Cultural relativism assumes not only social evolution but also human physical evolution.[78]

Situation Ethics

Situation ethics is found in two primary streams, atheistic and religious. The basic premise within this system is that love is the one norm or principle that is always binding and right.[79] In each and every situation requiring an ethical decision, all other principles and norms become subservient to the criterion of love. Situation ethics omits the idea of absolute moral principles, rather, any action that produces the greatest good for the greatest number is the loving thing to do. It is solely a utilitarian perception of love.

Situation ethics is the ethics of choice for many within contemporary culture. However, several logical difficulties are found within this ethical system that reveals its inadequacy.

(1)   It is self-contradictory. This view contends that there are no rules except the rule to love. But what if, in a certain situation, one decides that love is not the appropriate course of action? There are no absolutes in situation ethics—except that one absolutely must love in all situations! But what is the standard by which this mandate is defended?

(2)   In situational ethics love is purely subjective. In Joseph Fletcher's book, *Situation Ethics*, love is defined in no less than twelve ways. Who, then, decides what love is in any given context?

(3)   Situation ethics removes God as the moral sovereign of the universe, substituting man in his place. It completely ignores the biblical view that mere mortals are void of sufficient wisdom to guide their earthly activity (Jeremiah 10:23).

(4)   Love is defined as some sort of ambiguous, no-rule essence that is a cure-all for moral problems.[80]

Postmodernism

Postmodernism was discussed at length in Chapter 2. However, in terms of ethics, postmodernism is uniquely challenging. Postmodernism defines truth in subjective terms. Tolerance is expected of all because all belief systems are perceived as equally valid. The following characteristics reveal the inadequacy of postmodernism as an ethical system:

(1)   There is no grand purpose in life. The reason for living is to achieve comfortable survival.

(2)   Success is defined as the absence of pain and sacrifice, and the experience of happiness.

(3)   There is no value in focusing on or preparing for the future. Every person must live in the moment and for the moment.

(4)   There are no absolutes. All spiritual and moral principles are relative to the situation and the individual.

(5)   There is no omnipotent, all-knowing deity that guides reality. Each person must lean on his/her own vision, competencies, power and perceptions to make the most of life.[81]

Postmodernism poses two difficulties in particular. First, if all belief systems are equally valid, who determines truth when one or more systems collide? Second, if truth is subjective, what are the criteria that determine moral and ethical norms?

Scientific, Medical and Technological Advances

Scientific, technological and medical advances have created numerous benefits for contemporary society. They have also generated new and challenging ethical dilemmas.

> We are confronted by the greatest issues humankind has ever faced at a time when the moral fiber of our society appears to be at its weakest. Ethical questions are assaulting us at breakneck speed at a time when people have lost their sense of mooring, their sense of stability and their sense of possessing some platform on which to stand as they make moral decisions.[82]

Genetic engineering, gene therapy, stem cell research, fetal tissue research, cloning and genetic testing are a few modern advances that must be addressed. One example is in the area of genetic engineering where a cell's genetic structure is altered, with the promise of increased medical benefits. While the pursuit of medical advances is a noble objective, even here ethical questions arise, and the need for moral absolutes is evident.

Indeed, Christian ethics is confronted by the challenge of various ethical systems and ethical dilemmas. However, these challenges only serve to accentuate the validity and necessity of Christian ethics as the basis for life decisions and behavior.

Christian Ethics

The theological basis of Christian ethics originates within the biblical text. To validate this statement, biblical support is essential for each of the following six topics relating to Christian ethics: 1) nature; 2) basis; 3) source; 4) subjects; 5) goal; and 6) motive.

The Nature of Christian Ethics

At its core, unlike other ethical systems, Christian ethics is a system of absolutes. Absolute truth is universal and objective. It remains the same for every person in every culture in every generation. Christian ethics presupposes the existence of the one true God who has spoken to humankind by specific authoritative and eternal absolute truths. Christian ethics maintains the following absolutes:

(1)   Jesus declares, *I am the way and the truth and the life. No one comes to the Father except through me* (John 14:6). Jesus' declaration sets forth Christianity as the single and sole path to God.

(2)   An authority higher than humankind is revealed in Jesus. God's word as revealed in the Bible is paramount to all human reason, logic and philosophy.

(3)   The creator God is the absolute moral standard. This is a non-negotiable standard, eternally established in the immutable nature of God.

(4)   God's moral standard is timeless and exists for the well being of humankind.[83]

By its very nature Christian ethics requires the presence of absolutes. Anything less would invalidate the transcendent moral principles it sets forth.

The Basis of Christian Ethics

God's standard of morality is revealed in his Word. This is the basis of Christian ethics. *Who may ascend the hill of the LORD? Who may stand in his holy place? He who has clean hands and a pure heart, who does not lift up his soul to an idol or swear by what is false* (Psalm 24:3-4). Within this ethical system the criterion for moral decisions and conduct is the will of God as revealed in the Bible. Inherent in God's revealed will are the following basic ideas:

(1) God's moral revelation is based on His nature. God is separate from everything that exists, is free of all imperfections and limitations, and is His own standard. No moral rule exists outside of Him.

(2) God's moral principles have historical continuity. If God's moral revelation is rooted in His nature, it is clear that those moral principles will transcend time.

(3) God's moral revelation has intrinsic value. God's standards, like the laws of nature, have built-in consequences. Just as we have to deal with the laws of nature, we will eventually have to deal with the consequences of violating God's standards unless we put our faith in Christ.

(4) Obedience to God's Law is not legalism. The Bible speaks strongly against legalism since biblical morality is much more than external obedience to a moral code. No one can live up to God's standards without the enabling power of the Holy Spirit.

(5) God's moral revelation was given for the benefit of his people. Though in the short run it may sometimes appear that biblical moral standards are too restrictive, we can be sure that such injunctions are for our benefit because of His love for us.

(6) Exceptions to God's revelation must have biblical sanction. Our responsibility is to obey; God's responsibility is to take care of the consequences.[84]

The Source of Christian Ethics

Christian ethics finds its source in the person and nature of God. Concepts such as *good, bad, right* and *wrong* are essentially connected to the Christian view of God. The source of good choices and behavior is found in the one whose very nature is the essence of good. When the Scriptures differentiate between good and bad, the reader is directed to the nature of God.

Discovering what is right in a given situation requires the discernment of God's will. The fundamental mandate of Scripture is to imitate God. This position is corroborated in both the Old and New Testaments.

(1)   *I am the LORD your God; consecrate yourselves and be holy, because I am holy ... I am the LORD who brought you up out of Egypt to be your God; therefore be holy, because I am holy* (Leviticus 11:44-45).

(2)   *Do not conform to the evil desires you had when you lived in ignorance. But just as he who called you is holy, so be holy in all you do; for it is written: "Be holy, because I am holy"* (I Peter 1:14-16).

Understanding the source of Christian ethics is possible because God has revealed this aspect of his nature, while accentuating his attribute of holiness.

The Subject of Christian Ethics

Although God is intrinsically holy, the subject of Christian ethics involves that which is not holy, namely, humankind. The nature of humankind can be summed up in four statements:

(1)   Human beings are created beings.

(2)   Human beings are unique in creation.

(3)   Human beings are social creations.

(4)   Human beings are sinners. *All have sinned and fall short of the glory of God* (Romans 3:23).[85]

The subject of Christian ethics is to address these statements in a productive manner.

(1)   Human beings are not divine. As created beings there is a need for an ethical system that transcends that which is created.

(2)   Human beings are made in the image of God and comprise the pinnacle of the creative process. As such, human beings possess at least four qualities that distinguish them from the animals: 1) personality; 2) the ability to reason; 3) a moral nature; and 4) a spiritual nature.

(3)   As social creations human beings live in community. This requires a standard of conduct for promoting civil interaction within the community.

(4)   As sinners with a moral nature, human beings need an ethical system capable of transforming the sinful moral nature into that which is holy.[86]

The Goal of Christian Ethics

The ultimate objective of human existence is to bring glory to God. Scripture reveals that all persons are to *fear God and keep his commandments, for this is the whole duty of man* (Ecclesiastes 12:13). In addition, the Bible declares that *all the nations you have made will come and worship before you, O Lord; they will bring glory to your name* (Psalm 86:9). Jesus instructs his followers to, *Let your light shine before men in such a way that they may see your good works, and glorify your Father who is in heaven* (Matthew 5:16, NASB).

Lifestyle choices and behavioral patterns derived from a Christian ethic produce good works. These good works are visible displays of the God life. When observed by others these good works become a testimony to the enabling power of God. Ultimately, God is given the glory. Paul further validates this goal by asserting, *whether you eat or drink or whatever you do, do it all for the glory of God* (I Corinthians

10:31). By appropriating a Christian ethic as the basis for one's lifestyle and behavior, the primary objective is to bring God glory.

The Motive of Christian Ethics

The motivation to apply a Christian ethic is found primarily in one's love for God but also in one's love for fellow human beings. The Christian life is not designed to be lived in isolation, rather, it is a relationship with God and other people. The two are so intrinsically connected that they cannot legitimately be separated.

This motivation finds validation in the following passage: *If anyone says, "I love God," yet hates his brother, he is a liar. For anyone who does not love his brother, whom he has seen, cannot love God, whom he has not seen* (I John 4:20). In this verse, the motivation for Christian ethics is clearly identified—the vital relationship between love for God and love for others.

Problems in Christian Ethics

As an ethical system, Christian ethics is not without its concerns and criticisms. The following sampling will serve to highlight a few areas problematic for Christian ethics.

The Problem of Conflicts

Conflicts are inevitable within any ethical system. Christian ethics is not exempt. For example, if one's family is taken hostage with the only option for their release being the destruction of the captors, does one violate the prohibition of murder (Exodus 20:13) to save one's family? Or, does one violate the mandate to provide for and protect one's family (I Timothy 5:8), allowing the captors to kill them?

Several explanations have been suggested in addressing such conflicts:

(1)   God never puts us into a situation where we have to choose between commands. The conflict is only apparent and there is always a way to avoid sin. For example, Daniel and his three friends appear to be

in a dilemma when they are commanded to eat meat sacrificed to idols, a violation of their dietary code. Daniel presents his captors with a creative alternative, which allows him and his friends to honor their dietary code and meet the demands of the state at the same time.

(2)   A second approach is the lesser-of-two-evils view. There are genuine moral dilemmas with which one is faced in life where both alternatives are clearly wrong. In this situation, the lesser of the two evils is chosen, then, the sin is confessed.

(3)   A third option is called the "greater good" view. Those who hold this view claim it seems to be the model of Christ Himself. He spoke of *greater sin* (John 19:11), *greater love* (John 15:13), *greatest commandment* (Matthew 5:19), and *weightier matters* of the law (Matthew 23:23). It is one's duty to obey government, but not when in conflict with a command of God.[87]

The Problem of Evil

The existence of evil in the world, while simultaneously asserting the goodness of God, has deterred many sincere seekers from embracing the Christian faith. If God is omnipotent, then, why is there so much rampant evil in the world? If God is wholly good and wholly powerful, how does one account for the existence of evil? If He is all powerful, why does He not eliminate evil? If He is all good and the Creator of all that is, how did evil originate?

Resolving the concepts of good and evil has often been a daunting task for Christian ethicists and theologians. Perhaps the best approach in addressing this problem is to look to the Bible. The following three passages facilitate an understanding of the problem of evil:

(1)   Genesis 50:20: *You intended to harm me, but God intended it for good to accomplish what is now being done, the saving of many lives.* Here, God appears to allow evil to participate in His plan of redemption.

(2)   John 9:3: *Neither this man nor his parents sinned*, said Jesus, *but this happened so that the work of God might be displayed in his life.* Here, evil is allowed to ultimately reveal the glory of God.

(3)   Romans 9:17: For the Scripture says to Pharaoh: *I raised you up for this very purpose, that I might display my power in you and that my name might be proclaimed in all the earth.* Here, sin is permitted, yet God's sovereignty is intact.

The Problem of Interpretation

A third area that is problematic to Christian ethics is the area of interpretation. In seeking to interpret the Bible's ethical instructions and make them applicable to a particular setting, culture or situation, what role does human subjectivity play in the process? When interpreting the scriptures one must allow the text to speak for itself.

Interpretation also involves applying general ethical principles to specific life situations. For example, while the Bible does not specifically prohibit the recreational use of mind-altering drugs, it does indeed mandate the renewing of the mind through the offering of one's body as a living sacrifice to God (Romans 12:2). Consequently, one could argue that recreational drug use violates this mandate and should not be engaged in. A similar problem is found in the various ethical instructions that are best culturally interpreted. Paul's directive to greet one another with a holy kiss (Romans 16:16) could be applied in some cultures as greeting one another verbally or with a handshake.

While some areas of Christian ethics are indeed problematic, satisfactory resolutions to such concerns are available. Christian ethics sets forth a system of ethical principles and moral teachings that are unsurpassed in human history.[88]

Christian Ethics as an Adequate Ethical System

An adequate ethical system is a system that effectively addresses and engages the needs of a given context. Before discussing an adequate ethical system, it is important to understand what ethics is not.

(1)   Ethics is not the same as feelings.

(2)   Ethics is not following the law.

(3)   Ethics is not religion.

(4)   Ethics is not following culturally accepted norms.

(5)   Ethics is not science.[89]

The following components are key ingredients of an adequate ethical system: 1) a standard; 2) justice; 3) motive; 4) guidance or a model; 5) a relationship between rules and results; and 6) harmony. Christian ethics must also be evaluated in terms of these components.

The Need for a Standard

Inherent within an adequate ethical system is the necessity for a standard. A standard is a way of determining what qualifies an action or behavior as being right or wrong. It is a universal principle that transcends time and culture. A standard allows certain behaviors and actions to be determined as right or wrong, subsequently allowing one to make application in a given culture or context. Without a standard, ethics cannot adequately exist or operate.

Christian ethics qualifies as an adequate ethical system in this regard. To discover the rules of society that are best suited to nations there would need to exist a superior intelligence, who could understand the passions of men.[90] Indeed, this superior intelligence can be understood in an omniscient God. Within Christian ethics the very nature of God is the standard by which all moral conduct and behavior is defined. The essence of all that is good resides in the character of God. Jesus validates this truth by declaring, *No one is good—except God alone* (Mark 10:18). Emanating from the goodness of God is the standard for Christian ethics.

Because this standard is based upon God's holy nature, it is binding on all people. There is no standard beyond Him that can define moral conduct. Christian ethics applies to everyone, everywhere and in every context. God's moral revelation extends to all generations and is the ultimate standard for all human behavior.

The Need for Justice

The second major test of an adequate ethical system is the capacity to provide justice. Ethical justice can be understood from at least three perspectives. First, *restorative justice* focuses on the restoration of violated rights. Second, *remedial justice* focuses on the present correction of past injustices. Third, *retributive justice* focuses on future and final accountability.[91]

In each of these three perspectives the challenge is to provide justice on a consistent and comparable basis. Although many ethical systems fall short in this area, Christian ethics, correctly applied, provides adequate justice with equality. Regarding *restorative justice*, Christian ethics sets forth a principle that affirms the equality and dignity of all human beings. Paul asserts that for those in Christ and operating under a Christian ethic, *there is neither Jew nor Greek, slave nor free, male nor female, for you are all one in Christ Jesus* (Galatians 3:26-28). Regarding *remedial justice*, Christian ethics takes for granted that past injustices must be amended in the present. The result is that unjust behavioral patterns must change. Scripture validates this by asserting that *he who has been stealing must steal no longer, but must work, doing something useful with his own hands* (Ephesians 4:28). Regarding *retributive justice*, Scripture declares that at the future judgment, God will judge *every man according to their works* (Revelation 20:12). Christian ethics offers the assurance that all the failures of human justice will one day be totally rectified, and true justice will be meted out accordingly.[92]

The Need for a Motive

The third criterion of an adequate ethical system is motive. Motive may be defined as the source or reason behind a specific action.

Motives play a central role in ethics because they often carry the burden of … assessment. A [person] will be judged to have acted well or to be morally good as [he/she] acts from right motives … A [person] will be judged to have moral worth if [his/her] motive in acting is to conform [his/her] actions to the relevant principles of right or standard of goodness.[93]

For this reason more is needed than mere knowledge of correct moral behavior. There must also be the desire to act morally. Christian ethics provides an adequate motive to act morally. Although human beings are sinful by nature, after conversion the Holy Spirit encourages and enables the Christian to pursue moral behavior. Paul affirms this when he writes, *for it is God who works in you to will and to act according to his good purpose* (Philippians 2:13). The Holy Spirit motivates the believer in several areas. First, the new believer, indwelt by the Holy Spirit, is motivated by his love for God. This is what makes the believer want to obey God. Second, the Holy Spirit's confirmation of God's love for the believer motivates him to focus on the needs of others. Third, the believer is also motivated by external factors, such as the promise of eternal rewards.[94]

The Need for Guidance

The fourth ingredient of an adequate ethical system is guidance. How does one apply a particular ethical principle to a specific life situation? What process is needed to sort through any number of ethical principles and apply them accordingly? Herein lies the need for guidance to appropriate individual ethical principles. Inherent within Christian ethics is an adequate source of guidance that allows for successful application of ethical principles. To follow Christ implies that he leads and guides as one follows. Two examples in particular validate this aspect of Jesus' ministry:

(1)   Jesus beckons, *if anyone would come after me, he must deny himself and take up his cross and follow me* (Matthew 16:24).

(2)   Jesus states, *my sheep listen to my voice; I know them, and they follow me* (John 10:27).

Furthermore, guidance is a ministry of the Holy Spirit. Jesus said, *when he, the Spirit of truth, comes, he will guide you into all truth* (John 16:13). The believer also receives guidance from the Scriptures, which means that one should have a familiarity with the Word of God.

The Relationship between Rules and Results

Some ethical systems focus on rules, while others focus primarily on results. The fifth component of an adequate ethical system is a balanced relationship between rules and results. To arrive at a course of moral action, one would typically inquire as to the rules governing the type of action under consideration.[95] The goal of this approach is to determine *what is right*. The goal of result-oriented ethics is the effect. Within this approach good is determined primarily on the basis of the outcome.

Christian ethics sets forth a balance between rules and results. Scripture cautions against extreme positions in both areas. For example, Jesus denounced the extreme rule oriented approach of the Pharisees, yet he also taught that the end result of an action is insufficient in and of itself. One must have pure motives in the process of decision-making. Positive results do not guarantee the goodness of an action, however, in Christian ethics, it is reasonable for the Christian to assume that by following God-given rules the end result will be good.[96]

Internal Harmony

The sixth and final criterion of an adequate ethical system is internal harmony. Since it is inevitable that conflicts will occasionally arise, the various components of an adequate ethical system should function collectively with minimal internal conflict. Some ethical systems begin to implode when experiencing several opposing absolutes. Some argue that Christian ethics possesses this type of flaw, because whenever there is more than one absolute there will be hopeless conflict between absolutes.[97] Scripture, however, indicates otherwise. In an attempt to lure Jesus into using conflicting absolutes, the religious intellectuals of his time posed the following question:

> *"Teacher, which is the greatest commandment in the Law?"*
> *Jesus replied: "'Love the Lord your God with all your heart*
> *and with all your soul and with all your mind.' This is the*
> *first and greatest commandment. And the second is like*
> *it: 'Love your neighbor as yourself.' All the Law and the*
> *Prophets hang on these two commandments"* (Matthew
> 22:36-40).

Jesus responded by using two principles as though they were one. What appears initially to be a conflicting situation is resolved by applying a Christian ethical principle. Christian ethics teaches that all moral absolutes originate in the nature of God. Since the nature of God includes the attribute of omniscience, God who knows all things produces a harmony that will resolve potential conflicts within the system.[98]

Conclusion

The aim of this chapter was to offer a theological basis for Christian ethics and to evaluate Christian ethics in terms of the criteria needed for an adequate ethical system. While there is indeed the challenge of contemporary ethical systems, Christian ethics is shown to be adequate, far superior to the ethical systems of modern culture.

CHAPTER FIVE

An Analysis of I Timothy 4:16

After setting forth a biblical foundation for the Christian life and a theological basis for Christian ethics, the purpose of this chapter is to offer additional scriptural validation for the relationship between belief and behavior. Although several passages have already been noted, further examination of the biblical text is helpful. The immediate objective of biblical interpretation is to understand the biblical text, with the ultimate objective of applying that understanding to the contemporary church and world.[99] In this way the biblical text finds application to life and behavior. Once again, life and faith merge to form the basis for Christian living. A brief analysis of I Timothy 4:16 is offered based on this two-fold definition.

General Background of I Timothy

The letters (epistles) of I and II Timothy and Titus are typically referenced as a unit known as *the pastorals*. The three letters contain a shared emphasis on providing instruction in matters of doctrine and conduct. Within this general background and shared emphasis, I Timothy offers specific ethical guidelines. Internal evidence suggests the main theme of I Timothy is twofold: 1) sound doctrine; and 2) right living. Because false teachers were infiltrating the congregation at Ephesus, Timothy is frequently instructed to focus on correct doctrine (I Timothy 1:9-11; 3:9; 4:6; 6:3-4). He is then instructed to set an example in terms of conduct and behavior (I Timothy 4:12). Paul has three major purposes for writing to Timothy: 1) to encourage him to preserve the truth; 2) to instruct him to teach believers regarding Christian lifestyle and conduct; and 3) to command him to combat heresy.[100]

While many of the pastoral injunctions are personal in nature, a large portion of the ethical instruction is directed toward those to whom Timothy ministers.[101] An example is found in I Timothy 3:14-15, where Paul instructs Timothy to understand *how people ought to conduct themselves in God's household*. The context of the entire letter reinforces the relationship between doctrine and practice.

I Timothy 4:11-16

The New Testament letters are primarily comprised of individual small units of teaching and instruction. Before examining I Timothy 4:16 in particular, it will help to note the small unit within which it resides. I Timothy 4:11-16 is significant because it emphasizes the importance of Timothy's conduct in the discharge of his duties.[102] The text indicates that although Timothy is a young man, he is to set an example for his constituents regarding the following:

> *Don't let anyone look down on you because you are young, but set an example for the believers in speech, in life, in love, in faith and in purity. Until I come, devote yourself to the public reading of Scripture, to preaching and to teaching. Do not neglect your gift, which was given you through a prophetic message when the body of elders laid their hands on you. Be diligent in these matters; give yourself wholly to them, so that everyone may see your progress. Watch your life and doctrine closely. Persevere in them, because if you do, you will save both yourself and your hearers* (I Timothy 4:11-16).

This passage reinforces the theme reiterated throughout the letter—that Timothy is to appropriate a biblical ethic for the purpose of influencing his constituents toward godly living. He is to set an example through his godly lifestyle, personal conduct and moral character. This theme is reiterated throughout the New Testament not only for persons in leadership, but for all who are in a relationship with Christ through the New Covenant.

An analysis of verse 16 in particular is now offered. The analysis will focus on the following areas: 1) a comparative translation; 2) key words; and 3) synthesis.

Comparative Translation

A comparative translation of I Timothy 4:16 will be offered. Two approaches will be used: 1) a view of the verse in the original language; and 2) a review of three English translations. A comparative translation will then be offered.

(1)   UBS Greek New Testament
επεχε *[give heed]* σεαυτω *[to yourself]* και *[and]* τη *[to the]* διδασκαλια *[teaching;]* επιμενε *[continue]* αυτοις *[in them;]* τουτο γαρ *[for this]* ποιων *[doing,]* και *[and/both]* σεαυτον *[yourself]* σωσεις *[you will save]* και *[and/both]* τους *[those that]* ακουοντας *[hear]* σου *[you.]*[103]

(2)   New International Version
Watch your life and doctrine closely. Persevere in them, because if you do, you will save both yourself and your hearers.

(3)   New American Standard Bible
Pay close attention to yourself and to your teaching; persevere in these things, for as you do this you will ensure salvation both for yourself and for those who hear you.

(4)   New Living Translation
        Keep a close watch on how you live and on your teaching.
        Stay true to what is right for the sake of your own salvation
        and the salvation of those who hear you.

(5)   A Comparative Translation
        Watch your lifestyle and teaching very closely. Persevere in
        both. In doing this, you will save not only yourself but also
        those who hear you.

Key Words

I Timothy 4:16 is rather straightforward in its composition. Four key words enhance the meaning of the verse regarding its emphasis on biblical ethics: 1) watch; 2) life; 3) doctrine; and 4) persevere. Each word is briefly analyzed in terms of its definition and usage.

(1)   Watch
        The Greek verb επεχω is translated *watch* in this passage. Using the present active imperative tense, the implication is to *lay hold of, give attention to* or *watch closely.* Within the grammatical structure of the passage the subject of the verb is two-fold. Timothy's manner of life and accompanying teaching are intimately linked together.[104] Timothy is instructed to give special attention both to his behavior and belief system.

(2)   Life
        The first thing Timothy is told to watch is his life (σεαυτου). The word implies *yourself, your life* or *one's person.* Using the dative case, Timothy is instructed to continually watch and observe his manner of life. Paul is here emphasizing Timothy's crucial role as a model or pattern for the lives of others.[105] While written primarily to Timothy, the instruction is intended to address a broader audience, those to whom Timothy ministered.

(3) Doctrine

Timothy's second point of close observation is his doctrine (διδασκαλια). The word implies the *activity of a teacher* or *that, which is taught*. The primary usage here is in reference to the relatively fixed orthodoxy given to the churches, which they are to preserve against heresy.[106] Therefore, implied within the term is not only the aspect of *that which is taught* but also that which is accepted as truth. Timothy is to give special attention both to lifestyle and doctrine.

(4) Persevere

While watching closely his life and doctrine, Timothy is to persevere (επιμενε) in both. The present active imperative tense is used, meaning to *stay, remain, persist* or *continue in*. The implication here is not merely a brief examination of life and doctrine but a continual application.

Synthesis

Paul's purpose in I Timothy 4:16 is to accentuate the importance of both a godly lifestyle and orthodox doctrine. Here, good behavior is fundamentally connected with belief in doctrinal integrity. Timothy is to give heed to both, and in so doing set an example for those to whom he ministers. Paul's instructions in I Timothy 4:16 are written to Timothy as guidelines for successful and productive ministry. Timothy is encouraged to set an example for his parishioners by means of personal integrity, behavioral temperance and a godly lifestyle. His doctrine is to include the redemptive work of Christ as well as the moral and ethical instruction given by Paul. There is to be a continual examination of both behavior and belief for the purpose of advancing the effectiveness of his ministry and expanding the Kingdom of God on earth.

The instruction does not appear to be solely for Timothy. Although the letter is written primarily to Timothy, the letter's function is ultimately to offer ethical guidelines for the entire congregation.[107] This is vitally important to the issue of biblical ethics. In I Timothy 4:16, as well as in numerous other biblical passages, the fundamental relationship between belief and behavior is revealed. The directives set forth in I Timothy 4:16 are applicable to every follower of Christ. *Watch your life and doctrine closely. Persevere in them, because if you do, you will save both yourself and your hearers* (I Timothy 4:16). The essence of *saving oneself* is not the vicarious act of redemptive salvation. This was accomplished by Christ alone. It is rather a continual obedience to the commands of God—obedience that originates from a personal covenant relationship with the God of the Bible. This covenant relationship is the source of all ethical directives.

Indeed, the moral and ethical guidelines offered by Paul are not mere ideological assumptions to which mental assent is given. They are to be incorporated on a very practical level in the life of the believer. Biblical moral and ethical directives are the foundation upon which contemporary lifestyle and behavioral issues are to be determined and resolved.

> Behavior is influenced by core beliefs. It is possible to find changes in behavior without concurrent shifts in beliefs related to that behavior, but without change in the underlying beliefs, the changed behavior is not likely to remain changed. In most cases, the behavior will eventually revert back to its original state because there is not a mental, emotional and spiritual support system to sustain the alteration in activity.[108]

Because this is true, drifting from a committed Christian lifestyle based on biblical directives is dangerous to one's spiritual health and often disastrous to one's spiritual journey. Therefore, it is imperative that every Christian endeavor to pursue a balanced Christian life.

In Part I of the book the current state of affairs is explored. In Part II, an examination of biblical and theological foundations is offered. In Part III, the focus is on practical insight and guidelines for successfully pursuing a lifestyle pleasing to Christ.

PART THREE

EXPERIENCING THE FUSION

Chapter Six

Pursuing Biblical Guidelines

Christian ethics may indeed be examined, studied, researched and documented from a purely theoretical perspective. The premise of this book, however, is that Christian ethics involves much more than theory. The fundamental purpose of the theoretical aspects of Christian ethics is to engage life in some practical way. Wherever the practical application of Christian ethics occurs, it is at this point that life and faith meet. Indeed, there is a fusion of life and faith. Fusion is the merging of separate elements into a unified whole. This meeting place is the catalyst for successfully living the Christian life.

Spiritual growth occurs as Christians embrace and obey God's instructions for living.[109] For this reason, the principles set forth in this part of the book are of extreme importance. Biblical guidelines for Christian living, fellowship, service and worship are essential components for promoting spiritual growth and maturity in the life of the Christian. Each of these components is examined in Part III. A set of questions is included with each component that will allow further reflection regarding practical Christian living.

Spiritual Growth

The proclamation of God's Word is an important and essential aspect of spiritual growth. From its inception the church has used preaching and teaching to provide both personal and corporate instruction.[110] Paul instructs Timothy to devote himself *to preaching and to teaching* (I Timothy 4:13). He also notes that there are specific individuals within the church *whose work is preaching and teaching* (I Timothy 5:17). Those given the responsibility of preaching and teaching engage and influence the community of faith by: 1) warning of sin; 2) exhorting to do what is right; 3) caring for spiritual needs; 4) protecting from false teachers; and 5) equipping for local church ministry.[111]

Through preaching and teaching, spiritual growth is individually and corporately facilitated. Spirit-inspired preaching points people to God, subsequently encouraging them to a deeper level of Christian living. According to Paul, the components of preaching and teaching are designed

> to prepare God's people for works of service, so that the body of Christ may be built up until we all reach unity in the faith and in the knowledge of the Son of God and become mature, attaining to the whole measure of the fullness of Christ (Ephesians 4:11-12).

Although proclamation involves preaching, teaching and exhorting, the goal of these components is to make God's Word applicable to every area of life.[112] This is essential in producing spiritual growth.

The Sermon of Sermons

The ethical teachings of Jesus in Matthew chapters 5-7 comprise what is commonly known as the *Sermon on the Mount*.[113] Perhaps no other section of the gospels gives a more succinct and deliberate presentation of this new way of living introduced by our Lord. Jesus sets forth principles that, when appropriated, allow God's people, as salt and light, to have a powerful ethical influence upon culture. Jesus' sermon initiates the believer into a lifestyle that is pleasing to God.

Establishing New Standards

As Jesus introduces his ethical principles, he focuses primarily on setting forth new standards for human behavior. First, he deals with the individual. Although Jesus does not offer an exhaustive list, he addresses some of life's most fundamental issues. To the poor in spirit he promises the kingdom of heaven. To the mourners he assures them of comfort. To the meek he speaks of inheriting the earth. To the spiritually hungry he promises fulfillment. To the merciful he assures mercy. To the pure in heart he declares they will see God. To the peacemakers he gives the name sons of God. To the persecuted he affirms that heaven will be their ultimate reward.

Second, he focuses on the issue of influence. Jesus says, *you are the salt of the earth. But if the salt loses its saltiness, how can it be made salty again? It is no longer good for anything, except to be thrown out* (Matthew 5:13). In this passage, Jesus uses the quality and consistency of salt to describe the believer's capacity to influence his/her context. He warns his followers of the danger of empty ethics, a state in which the power of influence has been lost. Because influence is such an important aspect of Christian living, it is imperative that one's lifestyle and behavior be modeled after the ethical standards set forth by Jesus. Anything less negates one's capacity to be the kind of influence Jesus proposes.

Third, he speaks of infiltration. This is evident in Jesus' words, *you are the light of the world. A city on a hill cannot be hidden. Neither do people light a lamp and put it under a bowl. Instead they put it on its stand, and it gives light to everyone in the house. In the same way, let your light shine before men* (Matthew 5:14-16). The ability of light to illuminate the darkness vividly portrays Jesus' purpose for establishing a new ethic. Individuals with influence are instructed to infiltrate their world with the gospel. Consider the following questions and how they impact Christian living:

(1)   What does Matthew 5:13-16 teach about living a life pleasing to Christ?

(2)   What is the purpose of the beatitudes?

(3)   Since celebration is a key component in today's church, how can both celebration and concern for sin exist in the life of a believer?

(4)   Which of the beatitudes is most needed in your personal life?

(5)   What effect should the lives of godly people have on the church and on the world?

(6)   How can the attitude of the peacemaker encourage spiritual growth?

(7)   Since non-Christians notice the lives of believers, how can application of the beatitudes assist believers in leading non-Christians to Christ?

Emphasizing Scriptural Foundations

Jesus' sermon continues by emphasizing the scriptural foundations of his ethical teachings. He asserts that they are founded upon the truth of Scripture. Anything less is inadequate. Jesus proclaims himself as the embodiment of truth when he states, *I have not come to abolish them* [the Law or the Prophets] *but to fulfill them* (Matthew 5:17). A clear link is revealed between the ethical standards of the Old Testament and the new standards set forth by Jesus. As the Law calls for obedience to its numerous requirements, it also serves as a reminder that the ethics of Jesus call for obedience. His ethical guidelines do not mandate adherence to the Law but to the new way of living outlined in his teaching. Regarding this fact Jesus states, *unless your righteousness surpasses that of the Pharisees and the teachers of the law, you will certainly not enter the kingdom of heaven* (Matthew 5:20).

The relationship between Old Testament ethical guidelines and the new way of living is the essence of the remaining part of Matthew 5. This does not suggest that the Christian is bound by Old Testament guidelines; however, those guidelines do indeed serve as a foundation for the ethics of Jesus. In this part of the sermon, Jesus uses a form of instruction that, while emphasizing the scriptural foundation, expands the principle to accommodate the new way of living. Six times in these verses he uses the phrase, *you have heard…but I say*, and in so doing deals with the source of the problem. He establishes as a foundation the Old Testament prohibition on murder, then deals with uncontrolled anger—the primary source of murder. The same principle is used with adultery, where lust is revealed as the culprit. With divorce, he focuses on the breaking of covenant. Similarly, the breaking of oaths is viewed as a lack of integrity. Retaliation—*an eye for an eye*—is taken to its source, where bitterness is understood as the cause. Finally, regarding relationships, Jesus deals with the issue of selfish motivation. The following questions provide guidelines for reflection:

(1) Do you have the same love for the Old Testament as Jesus did?

(2) Should you embrace the laws of the Old Testament or Jesus' new way of life and behavior?

(3) Is there anyone for whom you feel extreme anger? If so, how can this be resolved?

(4) Does the fact that there should be no extended and unresolved conflict between believers mean that one must always agree with another believer?

(5) Do you ever consider engaging in wrong behavioral practices? What does Jesus think about it? What can you do to improve things?

(6) Is there any situation where telling a lie is acceptable?

(7) Should you forgive a thief who steals some expensive items from your home? Should you contact law enforcement? Should you do both?

Explaining Ethical Living

Matthew chapters 6-7 comprise the third section of Jesus' sermon. Here, Jesus identifies false lifestyles as a warning to his disciples. Jesus reveals that Christian ethics is not merely a set of beliefs but also an intentional effort to conform all personal conduct to the standard of

.s own righteousness. It is about dedicating one's whole life to God daily. At this point he attempts to explain this new way of living by setting forth concepts for life application.

First, he focuses on the disciplines of spiritual growth. Regarding giving, he states that it should be done discreetly, not with fanfare. Regarding personal prayer, he asserts that it is best accomplished in private communion. Regarding fasting, his instruction is to do so in a way that does not bring attention to the practice.

Second, Jesus addresses the issue of discernment. In so doing, he emphasizes the value of correct priorities. When one's priorities are in the right place, life is lived with an emphasis on spiritual and eternal matters. It isn't that material or temporal concerns aren't important, but they are not the most important things in life. Jesus reveals that the new way of living causes one to put God first in all matters, and as a result, God will indeed provide the material things that are needed.

Third, there is a focus on discrimination. Here, criticism is placed in practical terms. Jesus warns that the new way of living has no place for a judgmental attitude, and that the judgment of others brings a similar judgment to the one who is being judgmental. This type of judgment should be understood not as the biblical discernment of right and wrong (Hebrews 5:14) or the observation of fruit in the life of others (Luke 6:43-45) but as the intentional and deliberate finding of fault.

Jesus' sermon has established new standards, emphasized scriptural foundations, and explained ethical living. The sermon is not exhaustive in its content, but seeks to set forth criteria for making practical decisions for Christian living. At this point, the following questions allow for further reflection:

(1)   When you pray for something, do you really want God to answer you? If God does answer your requests, what changes will need to occur?

(2)   What are God's ambitions for you? Are you following them?

(3)   What do you think about discipline? Is discipline important?

(4)   What place should fasting have in the contemporary church?

(5)   Do some Christians tend to worry more than others? How can Christians help each other in this matter?

(6)   Since the doctrinal teaching in some churches today may be sincere, but false, what dangers are there in churches that teach false doctrine?

(7)   How can you know if someone's claim to be a Christian is true?

The Directive of Purity

The Old Testament mandates purity of life for the follower of God. *Consecrate yourselves and be holy, because I am the Lord your God* (Leviticus 20:7). This is not merely an archaic or outdated command. The New Testament mandates purity of life for Christians. *Just as he who called you is holy, so be holy in all you do* (I Peter 1:15). The directive is to a covenant relationship in which a particular quality of holiness is expected from the people of God.

The Call to Holy Living

The presence of willful, intentional and unforgiven sin in the body of Christ is a serious matter. Scripture validates this statement by calling the believer to holiness of life. In Romans 12:1, Paul introduces the principle of complete surrender to God for the purpose of living a consecrated lifestyle. He writes, *I urge you, brothers, in view of God's mercy, to offer your bodies as living sacrifices, holy and pleasing to God— this is your spiritual act of worship.*

First, Paul deals with the cause. He indicates the reason believers have been called to holy living. It is in view of something external, something totally separate from the believer—the mercy of God. Paul's urging is designed to validate this call. It is not presented as something optional but as an act of the will that is intentional and deliberate.

Second, the passage provokes a challenge. It is a challenge to give. Sincere reflection on the loving mercy of God elicits in the believer a desire to place at God's disposal not only one's intellect, emotions, desires and aspirations but also one's body. It is a total giving of one's self, the essence and entirety of one's person.

Third, there is the issue of consecration. Paul's use of the phrase *a living sacrifice* is indeed interesting. Offering one's body as a living sacrifice implies that every life situation is to be placed on the altar of God's will. It is the constant sacrifice of surrendering one's will and desires to God. A living sacrifice is constant devotion to serving God.

Fourth, Romans 12:1 highlights the conditions. The living sacrifice is to be holy—something set apart, something pure and consecrated, and fully pleasing to God. In fulfilling these conditions—living a holy life before God—the believer is rendering a spiritual act of worship. It is noteworthy that Paul equates holy living with worship. Why? Worship is often understood within the context of community, for example, worship services, praise events, and similar venues. Here, worship is defined in very personal terms. The following questions will assist in personalizing the call to holy living:

(1) What characterizes a life that is out of fellowship with God?

(2) Since the call to holy living is a call to separate oneself from sinful living, what is the result of sin in one's life?

(3) Has the presence of sin in your life ever affected your relationship with God?

(4) Are you willing to ask God to reveal any areas of sinful practice or behavior in your life that would displease him? If so, how will you respond to those things God may reveal?

(5) In what ways can you offer yourself as a living sacrifice to God?

(6) Does God require holy living for all Christians or only for those serving in positions of leadership and influence?

(7)   How can a godly lifestyle facilitate leading others to Christ?

The Commitment to Holy Living

In Romans 12:1, a clear call to holy living is given. In Romans 12: 2, Paul reinforces the need for a commitment to holy living. In this passage, he cautions the believer regarding conformity to the world system. Paul writes, *do not conform any longer to the pattern of this world, but be transformed by the renewing of your mind. Then you will be able to test and approve what God's will is—his good, pleasing and perfect will.* He then transitions to the mandate of being transformed into the image of Christ, which can only occur as one is committed to holy living.

First, the emphasis is on outward conformity. The believer is not to be conformed to the pattern of this world. While not an exhaustive treatment of the subject, this certainly references the world's model of living with all its promises, hopes and dreams. It also speaks to the world's morals, which are more often than not diametrically opposed to biblical morality. The world's obsession with materialism is of concern at this point. There is to be no conformity to these standards of living by the believer.

Second, there is a clear directive toward inward transformation. If one is to successfully fulfill the mandate of not conforming to the pattern of the world, one must experience the transforming power of a renewed mind. The renewing of the mind is a committing of one's spirit (emotions), soul (intellect), and body (behavior) to the will of God. This is not a singular act but a progressive ongoing aspect of holy living.

Third, the believer is encouraged to an upward emulation. As the mind is being transformed the believer is given the ability to test and to prove God's will for his/her life. The following questions will assist in the process:

(1)   Because sin gives Satan a stronghold in one's life, have you confessed all known sin in your life?

(2)   Have you centered your affections on Christ and surrendered to his Lordship?

(3)   Have you, through an act of your will by faith, been made free in Christ?

(4)   Are you walking in the Spirit, living in the Spirit, and asking to be filled with the Spirit on a daily basis?

(5)   Are you studying God's Word every day?

(6)   Are you experiencing the power of prayer every day?

(7)   Are you living by faith on a daily basis?

The Criteria for Holy Living

Any suggested model requires specific criteria for accomplishing particular objectives. Criteria for holy living are found in I Peter 2, where guidelines are provided to assist in practical decision-making. As in other passages, this chapter does not offer an exhaustive treatment of the issue but sets forth in general terms guidelines for holy living.

First, Peter introduces the concepts of renouncing and receiving. The believer is to renounce *all malice and all deceit, hypocrisy, envy, and slander of every kind* (2:1). Believers must then, *like newborn babies, crave pure spiritual milk, so that by it [they] may grow up in [their] salvation* (2:2-3).

Second, there is an emphasis on relationships. There is the relationship between the Father and Son in which Jesus is *rejected by men but chosen by God* (2:4). This becomes the model by which the relationship between Christ and believers is defined. Peter writes, *you…like living stones, are being built into a spiritual house to be a holy priesthood, offering spiritual sacrifices acceptable to God* (2:5).

Third, the passage addresses the issue of respect. One criterion for holy living is a compliance with secular and civil authorities. Peter writes, *submit yourselves for the Lord's sake to every authority instituted among men* (2:13). This does not suggest compliance to activities or behavior prohibited in Scripture but an ability to work for the good of the community-at-large.

Fourth, Peter lifts up the importance of a role model in the pursuit of holy living. Jesus is presented as the supreme role model. He writes, *to this you were called, because Christ suffered for you, leaving you an example, that you should follow in his steps. He committed no sin and no deceit was found in his mouth* (2:21-22). An adequate role model will assist in reaching the objective of holy living. The following questions will offer insight in this area for practical application:

(1)   Who is your model in making decisions?

(2)   Will this decision compromise your faith and commitment to God?

(3)   Since all decisions have consequences, will this decision ultimately bring glory to God?

(4)   How will this decision affect others?

(5)   Is this decision fair to everyone involved?

(6)   How will this decision affect your standard of integrity?

(7)   Will this decision enable you to live a lifestyle that pleases God?

Conclusion

The three chapters that comprise Part III of this book specifically highlight the practical aspect of Christian ethics. How does one cause life and faith to meet? Here, the intention is to facilitate the process of reaching that meeting place. Questions for reflection are offered in order to add practical and personal facets to the process. In this chapter the pursuit of biblical guidelines for Christian living was discussed. In the next chapter there is a logical movement to address the question, "How now shall we live?"

Chapter Seven

How Then Shall We Live?

As noted in previous chapters, contemporary society has no shortage of paths to enlightenment. With so many paths viewed as legitimate routes to God, with each claiming to have all the answers, how then shall we live? How does one cause life and faith to meet? Building on his Anglican theological tradition, John Wesley set forth what he believed to be the four core components for Christian living: Scripture, tradition, reason, and experience. He taught that Scripture is the primary source and standard for Christian doctrine. Tradition is the development and growth of the faith through the past centuries and in various nations and cultures. Through reason the Christian brings discernment to the Christian faith. Experience enables one to understand and appropriate the faith in one's own life. These four elements taken together lead the Christian into a mature and fulfilling understanding of the Christian faith and the required response of fellowship, service and worship.[114]

The component of Scripture, the ultimate source of all Christian living, is absolutely necessary in all areas where one must determine practical issues of lifestyle and behavior. The positive aspects of one's faith tradition are available to be drawn from as needed. The element of reason—the capacity whereby one is able to discern God's will in a given matter—is constantly being developed through the practice of spiritual

...iplines. Through experience the previous components merge into a cohesive unit designed for living out the faith. These components, when pursued with tenacity, encourage the Christian to respond in ways that allow life and faith to meet. This chapter highlights three of those merging points: fellowship, service and worship.

Fellowship

The first merging point of life and faith is fellowship. One of the traits of the early church is recorded in Acts 2:42. Luke records that those early followers of Jesus *devoted themselves...to the fellowship* [*koinonia*]. The term *koinonia*, as used here, describes more than superficial human interaction. It is used to illustrate the following relational components: 1) fellowship with Christ (I Corinthians 1:9); 2) fellowship with the Holy Spirit (II Corinthians 13:14); 3) partnership in the gospel (Philippians 1:5); and 4) sharing the faith (Philemon 6).[115]

This concept of fellowship is further validated in the following observation:

> Fellowship involves more than a communal spirit that believers share with one another. It is a joint participation at the deepest level in a spiritual fellowship that is in Christ. On the human side believers share with one another, but the quality of their fellowship is determined by their union with Christ.[116]

Fellowship is essential for healthy spiritual growth. This type of growth is achieved through understanding and walking in the light of God's Word. One's growth in fellowship with God enriches one's fellowship with other believers; thereby facilitating the spiritual growth in others by one's example and ministry to them.[117] As believers mature in their fellowship with Christ, it is manifested through interpersonal relationships with others. This, in turn, facilitates the process of spiritual growth, subsequently influencing Christian behavior and lifestyle. The biblical concept of fellowship may be understood as:

(1)   A close association involving mutual interests and sharing (I Corinthians 1:9; Acts 2:42)

(2)   An attitude of goodwill that manifests an interest in a close relationship (Hebrews 13:16; II Corinthians 9:13)

(3)   A sign of fellowship or proof of brotherly unity (Romans 15:26)

(4)   Participation and sharing (Philemon 6; Philippians 3:10)[118]

Using the above definitions, biblical fellowship has two objectives: 1) to promote spiritual growth in the Christian life; and 2) to promote accountability.

Small Groups

Although this section of the chapter is titled *Small Groups*, the use of this term should be expanded to include any or all of the following: cell groups, one-on-one peer groups, accountability partners, small Bible study groups. Such groups are designed to promote spiritual growth in the Christian life by incorporating intimacy, interaction, and accountability. Each of these is an essential component of fellowship (Matthew 5:14-16; John 4:34-38; 6:43-45). Such groups are designed to

> provide the framework for people to...have a life that is triumphant and joyful, fulfilling and exciting, and rewarding in that we become the blessed to be a blessing to those around us.[119]

When properly implemented, participants are able to foster both an understanding and application of biblical passages relating to the Christian lifestyle. The small groups should be planned to meet periodically and consistently for a designated period of time. The following format is one of many that can be used as is, amended or adapted for the particular needs of participants.

I.   Prayer
II.   Reading
        A. Preselected passages
        B. Scripture relating to Christian living
        C. One designated passage per week
III.   Rumination
        A. What does it say?
        B. What does it mean?
        C. What is God telling me?
        D. How can I be changed to learn and grow?
IV.   Reflection
        A. Listen to each member of the group
        B. State what the group is not about
        C. Reinforce the purpose of the group
V.   Refocusing
        A. What is the key to spiritual growth?
        B. How can this passage change me?
VI.   Resources
        A. Listening is essential
        B. Allowing dialogue
VII.   Prayer

Accountability

The second objective of fellowship is to cultivate accountability among the people of God. As with small group interaction, the purpose is to promote spiritual growth. Accountability is a biblical concept promoted in both the Old and New Testaments. Examples of accountability can be found in the following passages: Proverbs 25:12; 27:17; Ecclesiastes 4:8-12; Romans 14: 13-23; and Hebrews 3:13). Accountability

> allows us to be answerable to one another, with the focus on improving our key relationships…Accountability will also enhance our integrity, maturity, character, relationships, and our growth in Christ.[120]

Small group participants are asked to choose an accountability partner—one whom he or she knows to be reliable, responsible and dependable. The purpose is to share in the process of spiritual growth. Colleagues are encouraged to communicate once per week, preferably in person, for the purpose of fostering accountability. If person-to-person meetings are not possible, e-mail or phone contact is satisfactory. The following questions serve as general guidelines (that may be adapted or expanded) for developing and maintaining accountability:

(1)   Are you dealing with specific concerns?

(2)   What is God doing in your life now?

(3)   What is preventing Him from working in you?

(4)   How is your Bible reading and study going?

(5)   How is Satan trying to work in your life?

(6)   What temptations/sins are you experiencing?

(7)   How are you seeking to resolve them?

Service

The second merging point of life and faith is service. Service (*diakonia*) is especially oriented to Christian living. The term's usage in the New Testament is understood from three perspectives:

(1)   The waiting of tables or provision for bodily sustenance

(2)   The discharging of a service

(3)   The discharging of particular obligations to the community[121]

Personal involvement in some form of Christian service fulfills the law of Christ. Jesus personifies this teaching when he states, *whatever you did for one of the least of these brothers of mine, you did for me* (Matthew 25:40). This verse emphasizes that Christian service has a biblical foundation. Every form of the term service finds its ultimate meaning and fulfillment in the collective unity of the body of Christ (Romans 12:7).[122]

Service is especially important as a means of spiritual growth. Paul writes in Galatians 5:13, *do not use your freedom to indulge the sinful nature; rather, serve one another in love.* This aspect of service belongs to every believer, and includes the following basic principles: 1) praying (John 14:13); 2) consistent Christian living (I Peter 1:15); 3) giving (Ephesians 4:28); and 4) witnessing (Acts 1:8)[123] Furthermore, Christian service is the result of obedience to the mandate of God's Word. Obedience inevitably leads to sanctification and spiritual growth in the life of the believer (Romans 6:16, 19, 22). Service may be rendered within the church and outside the church. Both are vitally important.

Service Within the Church

Each believer is asked to choose one area of service and commit to serve in that area for a minimum of one month. Following is a brief list of possible areas of service:

(1)   Library

(2)   Office

(3)   Nursery

(4)   Media

(5)   Building and grounds maintenance

(6)   Custodial services

(7)   Bus and van

(8)   Senior adults

(9)   Youth

(10)   Food and clothing pantry

(11)   Usher/greeter

(12)   Music

Once an area of service is selected, one should serve under the guidance of the ministry leader in the chosen area. Primary accountability is to the ministry leader who will serve as a mentor by providing the following:

(1)   A biblical basis for ministry in the chosen area

(2)   Hands-on instruction for effective service

(3)   Opportunities for service

(4)   Feedback, interaction, and encouragement

(5)   Prayer

Through discipline, sacrifice and a spirit of humility, believers are encouraged to assume the posture of a servant, thus exemplifying the model of Christ (John 13). Focusing on the needs of others within the family of faith will assist in engendering commitment and fostering spiritual growth.

Service Outside the Church

The Great Commission as recorded in Matthew 28:18-20 challenges believers to *go and make disciples of all nations.* The implication of this mandate is, *as you go, participate in expanding the kingdom of God on earth.* This aspect of Christian service is personal in nature. Part of the mandate, *as you go,* is primarily connected with one's individual context. The context of contemporary believers is characterized by the following traits of postmodernism (See Chapter 2):

(1)   Rejection of divine authority

(2)   Religious relativism

(3)   Moral instability

(4)   Social and political fragmentation

(5)   Pragmatism

While the above traits negatively impact the context, they also provide the opportunity for participation in the Great Commission. Postmodern culture lends itself to the power of story—focusing on narrative presentations of faith.[124] Believers are encouraged to participate in the Great Commission by using the narrative approach. This approach has its origin in the scriptural admonition to *always be prepared to give an answer to everyone who asks you to give the reason for the hope that you have* (I Peter 3:15).

Using the *as you go* mandate as a reference point, believers are encouraged to pray and look for specific opportunities to share their story with unbelieving relatives, friends and acquaintances. Examples of this approach are listed below, as believers are encouraged to share their story:

(1) Take the initiative in the conversation

(2) Talk to people one-on-one

(3) Engage in dialogue rather than monologue

(4) Present the story incrementally

(5) Make the most of split-second opportunities.

(6) Pray for the Holy Spirit to present opportunities[125]

Three primary aspects of the story should be understood and utilized as the Holy Spirit provides opportunity for sharing.

(1) Pre-conversion (Acts 26:4-11)
     What was your early spiritual background, and how did it affect you as you grew up—your feelings, attitudes, actions, and relationships? What caused you to begin to consider following Christ? Share this with the person to whom you are speaking.

(2) Conversion (Acts 26:12-18)
     What realization did you come to that finally motivated you to receive Christ? Specifically, *how* did you receive Christ? Share this with the person to whom you are speaking.

(3)   Post-conversion (Acts 26:19-23)
How did your life begin to change after you trusted Christ? What other benefits have you experienced since becoming a Christian? Share this with the person to whom you are speaking.

Take advantage of opportunities for service. Be intentional. The believer's commitment to Christian living is ultimately strengthened by doing so.

Worship

The third merging point of life and faith is worship (*leitourgia*). One of the most elementary functions of the believer is to render worship to God. Both Old and New Testaments declare the importance of worship. *Worship the Lord in the splendor of his holiness* (Psalm 29:2). *True worshipers will worship the Father in spirit and truth* (John 4:23). Genuine worship includes the following essentials:

(1)   Reverence and awe

(2)   Praise and thanksgiving

(3)   Humility and contrition

(4)   Supplication and intercession

(5)   Consecration and dedication[126]

Worship is both a personal and corporate exercise. Worship occurs on a personal level when one renders to God praise and exaltation from the heart. In corporate settings the entire body of believers participates in the rendering of worship. Worship can be described primarily as a response by people to the awesome nature of God. Through worship, the primary question people ask themselves is: "Did I meet God?"[127]

Worship as a Means of Spiritual Growth

It is clear that genuine worship facilitates the process of spiritual growth. Worshiping God according to biblical guidelines inevitably leads to spiritual growth, development and maturity in the life of the believer. This occurs by incorporating the following essentials:

(1)   One should examine his/her life for any known sin that needs to be dealt with through repentance and confession.

(2)   One should give his/her self to the Holy Spirit for his direction.

(3)   One should render gratitude for the privilege of worshiping God.

(4)   One should have the confidence that God will accept his/her spiritual sacrifices.[128]

Why is worship so important? Genuine worship relieves the stress of everyday life by replacing fear, doubt and hopelessness with faith, assurance and affirmation. This type of worship inevitably leads to maturity in the life of the believer. Practical application of the above criteria is seen in two areas: 1) worship in song; and 2) worship through godly living.

Worship in Song

The first area of practical application is worship in song. It is important to promote personal consecration to Christ by encouraging worship in song. Such worship includes but is not limited to: 1) expressions of gratitude for the privilege of worshiping God; and 2) confidence in God's acceptance of our spiritual sacrifices. Although many Christians participate in congregational singing, few have discovered the joy of one of the most neglected aspects of personal worship—singing alone in God's presence.[129] This practice finds biblical precedent in Psalm 100:2, where the psalmist instructs the reader to *worship the LORD with gladness; come before him with joyful songs.*

Believers are encouraged as part of their daily devotional practice to incorporate singing unto the Lord as an act of worship. Believers are encouraged to set aside a particular time each day for the purpose of personal worship. Following are examples of how this may be accomplished:[130]

(1) Pause in the devotional time to sing a specific song unto the Lord.

(2) Select a special theme for the song. The Psalms offer at least six distinct themes for singing unto the Lord:

- Songs of praise
  Praise the LORD, for the LORD is good; sing praise to his name, for that is pleasant (Psalm 135:3)

- Songs of power and mercy
  I will sing of your strength, in the morning I will sing of your love; for you are my fortress, my refuge in times of trouble (Psalm 59:16)

- Songs of thanksgiving
  Sing to the LORD with thanksgiving (Psalm 147:7)

- Songs of God's name
  I will praise God's name in song and glorify him with thanksgiving (Psalm 69:30)

- Songs of God's word
  Your decrees are the theme of my song wherever I lodge (Psalm 119:54)

- Songs from the heart
  I will sing a new song to you, O God (Psalm 144:9)

(3) Ask the Holy Spirit to create new melodies in your heart so your song is truly a *new song*.

(4) Don't hesitate to sing songs of thanksgiving for your specific blessings or victories you believe God has given or will give.

(5) Sing songs and hymns that promote personal consecration to Christ.

Worshiping in song enhances the relationship between God and the believer. This ultimately creates a desire to incorporate the will of God in one's life and behavior.

Worship through Godly Living

The second area of practical application is worship through godly living. True worship is worship that is biblically correct and cultivates purity of life and behavior. The words of Psalm 15:1-5 clearly support this assertion:

> *LORD, who may dwell in your sanctuary? Who may live on your holy hill? He whose walk is blameless and who does what is righteous, who speaks the truth from his heart and has no slander on his tongue, who does his neighbor no wrong and casts no slur on his fellowman, who despises a vile man but honors those who fear the LORD, who keeps his oath even when it hurts, who lends his money without usury and does not accept a bribe against the innocent. He who does these things will never be shaken.*

Worship through godly living requires participation on the part of the believer. First, one must examine one's life for any willful, continual and known sin. If areas of sinful behavior are found, these areas must be dealt with through confession and repentance. They must be properly addressed. When one fails to properly address such areas, they become obstacles to one's spiritual growth and development. Second, one must surrender all aspects of one's life to the direction of the Holy Spirit. In so doing, the believer is empowered to live a victorious life. How is this possible? *The one who is in you is greater than the one who is in the world* (I John 4:4).

Paul endorses the idea that godly living is indeed an act of worship. In Romans 12:1 he asserts that offering one's body as a living sacrifice to God becomes a *spiritual act of worship*. Since genuine worship has such a positive impact on one's behavior and lifestyle, believers are encouraged to implement the following practical guidelines:

(1)   Worship through prayer
    Think about the issues you usually pray about. How much of your prayer life is about you and how much of it is about God? God wants us to be able to share

everything that is going on in our life. But he also wants us to get to know him better.

(2)   Develop a regular habit of reading the Bible
The Bible says we worship God in spirit and in truth. How can we ever worship God without a clear understanding of who he is? Knowing the truth about God is essential to worship. Pay special attention to the book of Psalms.

(3)   Obey God
Christians need to build the habit of obedience into our lives. Take practical steps to see that this is a part of your life. Whenever you sense God is speaking to you, make it a regular practice to respond immediately. Don't let procrastination weigh you down.

(4)   Tithe
The Bible teaches the important lesson that *where your treasure is, there your heart will be also* (Matthew 6:21). God wants us to surrender our entire being to him. One way to show our dedication is by making him Lord of our finances. If you are already a committed tither, look for missions' projects to give toward, in addition to your tithe.

(5)   Build deep relationships with other Christians
The Bible teaches that God designed us to live in community with other Christians. We bring God pleasure by getting to know others and being known by them.

(6)   Build into your life the attitude of thankfulness
This requires looking at the world through a different set of eyes. When we look through the lens of thankfulness, we see our lives as gifts from God. Develop your own spiritual exercise of thanking God each morning for all of the good things in your life.

(7)   Make a complete surrender to God
The heart of worship is total surrender to God. You might have been a follower of Jesus for years, but you still have areas of your life that you are holding back from Him. What are those areas? Do they honor God?

(8)   Live a life of purpose
God has a reason for your existence. In fact, he has five specific reasons: fellowship, discipleship, ministry, evangelism and worship. We please God when we live in step with his purpose.[131]

Conclusion

How then shall we live? This chapter offers specific guidelines promoting a Christian lifestyle. The guidelines may be amended or adapted to work within a given context. The guidelines are not exhaustive; however, they do indeed offer a merging point for a life of faith—a place where life and faith can meet and where one may pursue with diligence the heart of God.

Chapter Eight

Where Life and Faith Meet

A Biblical Worldview

As revealed in the survey discussed in Chapter 1, there is a need among Christians in general to understand and apply a biblical worldview in matters of life and faith. But what is a worldview and why is it so important? A worldview is a way of looking at the world. It is a lens through which one perceives life with all its many facets. Worldviews have consequences upon the life and behavior of their adherents. Contemporary culture is daily affected and influenced by them.[132]

Several worldviews are discussed briefly in Chapter 1—materialism, hedonism, atheism, individualism, humanism and pragmatism. Definitions for each are given in that chapter. Each offers guidelines for living and its own system of ethics. Of course, each of the worldviews is inadequate as it relates to Christian living. For this reason, it is imperative that believers understand a biblical worldview and live their lives within the parameters of that worldview. How does one accomplish this objective?

A worldview provides a mental filter that influences everything related to one's perspective on life, truth, and meaning.[133] Applying this definition to a biblical worldview enhances one's understanding of why it is so important to successful Christian living. *A biblical worldview—which finds its origin in the Word of God—influences everything related to one's perspective on life, truth, and meaning.* Specifically, a biblical worldview influences one's lifestyle and behavior. To facilitate the process of spiritual growth in this area, the following questions provide guidelines for study, reflection, and application:

(1)   What is truth?

(2)   Can you define a biblical worldview?

(3)   Do we really need a biblical worldview?

(4)   Are people held accountable for their worldview?

(5)   How does a biblical worldview influence one's belief system?

(6)   How does a biblical worldview affect one's behavior and lifestyle?

(7)   How can a biblical worldview facilitate winning the lost to Christ?

(8)   Do all values and rights originate in the individual? If not, how does one determine right and wrong?

(9)   Is the pursuit of happiness and pleasure the ultimate goal in life? If not, what is the ultimate goal in life?

(10)   How does one make sense of all the pain and suffering in the world?

(11)   What is the meaning of life? Why am I here? What is my purpose?

(12)   Is it possible to make moral decisions apart from the Bible? What makes the Bible more valid than other religious writings?

The purpose of this section is to emphasize the importance of understanding, pursuing, and maintaining a biblical worldview. When decisions are made based on a biblical worldview, the outcome is one that pleases God.

Exemplary Living

Christian ethics is the means whereby life and faith meet. Lifestyle and behavioral decisions based on Christian ethics allow for the fusion of life and faith in the lives of individual believers. The believer becomes a letter, *known and read by everybody* (II Corinthians 3:2). For this reason exemplary living should be the goal of those who follow Christ. Some emphasize Christian liberty to the point of negating all accountability. In their way of thinking, any suggestion of lifestyle guidelines is perceived as legalism. In contrast, others are so dictatorial in their approach to Christian living, most everything is perceived as sinful. Neither extreme is biblical and both are harmful.

The following topics represent broad areas of the Christian life. Decisions are made daily in each area that impact the believer's life—both positive and negative. The principles set forth in each area do not attempt to legislate moral conduct or behavior, nor do they constitute an exhaustive treatment of the subject. Rather, the principles serve as guidelines for a lifestyle based on Christian ethics. A brief explanation is given in each area, along with a set of questions for further reflection.[134]

Family

Before God established a nation, a kingdom, or even the church, he instituted the family. The family is the basic unit of human relationship and, as such, is foundational to both society and the church. Christian ethics calls for the believer to give priority to family responsibilities, preserve the sacredness of marriage, and maintain divine order in the home. Early in the narrative of Scripture, God's perception of the family is revealed. He states, *it is not good for the man to be alone. I will make a helper suitable for him* (Genesis 2:18). From the beginning of human history, God's order for the family is established in a monogamous heterosexual union. Validation for this is found in Genesis 2:24, *For this reason a man will leave his father and mother and be united to his wife, and they will become one flesh.* This sacred union—one flesh—is known as marriage, a spiritual union in which a man and woman are joined by God.

When God creates humankind, he creates male and female. *God created man in his own image, in the image of God he created him; male and female he created them* (Genesis 1:27). He gives each gender different characteristics and responsibilities. In so doing, he establishes divine order within the family unit; therefore, it is imperative that believers follow God's ordained pattern of human relationship. It is here, in the most fundamental of human institutions, that exemplary living begins. The following questions provide guidelines for reflection:

(1) From the biblical account of creation, what are some of the major points one should understand regarding the family?

(2) What are the biblical reasons for marriage?

(3) Why should one regard the family as God's most fundamental institution?

(4) What are the responsibilities of the husband?

(5) What are the responsibilities of the wife?

(6) What is the relationship between parents and children?

(7) In what ways, if any, does the family impact the church?

Example

The Christian is in a strategic position to influence his/her environment. Jesus uses the analogy of salt, light, and yeast to describe the capacity of the Christian to make a difference. In a world that so desperately needs spiritual healing, the Christian stands as a beacon of hope. In simple terms the Christian is an example. This truth carries a tremendous responsibility, because each believer is accountable for the type of example he/she portrays. Exemplary living calls for an example that points others to Christ. Several areas of discussion will help highlight the importance of this reality.

First, the believer is called to a lifestyle that incorporates spiritual disciplines. The believer is a potent influence when the elements of prayer, praise, fasting, and meditation are incorporated into the lifestyle and behavioral patterns (Matthew 6:5-15).

Second, the believer is an influence when there is a sense of purpose in his/her life. The Christian faith presupposes a responsibility to the body of Christ. Because this is true, believers are to unite regularly with other members of the church. Scripture validates this in the admonition, *let us not neglect…meeting together, as some people do, but encourage one another, especially now that the day of his return is drawing near* (Hebrews 10:25, NLT).

Third, the believer is an influence regarding stewardship. Scripture prohibits waste yet promotes prudence in one's lifestyle. *Store your treasures in heaven, where moths and rust cannot destroy, and thieves do not break in and steal* (Matthew 6:20, NLT). The following questions provide guidelines for reflection:

(1) According to I Timothy 4:12, in what specific ways did Paul instruct Timothy to be a spiritual example?

(2) What biblical guidelines should be followed in order to promote being a spiritual example?

(3) Does God require all Christians to be a spiritual example or only those serving in leadership?

(4) Does each Christian have a responsibility to his or her fellow believers?

(5) As a basis for spiritual example, what strengths and weaknesses do you see in your personal life?

(6) Is faithfulness in church attendance important to one's spiritual example?

(7) How does one's spiritual example or lack thereof impact one's capacity to lead others to Christ?

Purity

As noted in Chapter 6, the Christian life is a call to purity. Holiness, sanctification, righteousness—each of these terms emphasize the importance of purity in one's life. This area of Christian living is often the source of legalism, fanaticism, and harshness on the part of some. For this reason, many decline to address the subject matter. Consequently, there is often no clear understanding of its importance. The Christian is called to engage in activities that bring glory to God. *Whether you eat or drink or whatever you do, do it all for the glory of God* (I Corinthians 10:31).

First, purity involves the body. Paul writes, *Your body is the temple of the Holy Spirit, who lives in you...You do not belong to yourself...So you must honor God with your body* (I Corinthians 6:19-20). As the temple of the Holy Spirit, one's body is to be used in a way that does not violate scriptural prohibitions.

Second, purity involves that which is allowed to enter the body by way of the mind. The mind is an entrance to one's inner person. Because this is true, one should read, watch and listen to those things that inspire and challenge one to a higher plane of living. *Fix your thoughts on what is true, and honorable, and right, and pure, and lovely, and admirable. Think about things that are excellent and worthy of praise* (Philippians 4:8, NLT).

Third, purity involves those things one views as entertainment. Christian ethics certainly allows for entertainment, relaxation and recuperation from the stress of life. However, all activities and entertainment chosen by the believer are to edify and promote spiritual health. Participation in morally and ethically questionable activities are to be avoided. *Do not let any part of your body become an instrument of evil to serve sin. Instead, give yourselves completely to God, for you were dead, but now you have new life. So use your whole body as an instrument to do what is right for the glory of God* (Romans 6:13, NLT). The following questions provide guidelines for reflection:

(1) What relationship do you see between today's moral climate and the contemporary attitude regarding morality?

(2)   To what extent, if any, does the current moral climate affect the lives of Christians?

(3)   What do you see as the most serious consequences of the declining moral standards?

(4)   How would you constructively address the problem(s) identified in question number 3?

(5)   Why is it important to have a correct understanding of moral purity?

(6)   What relationship do you see between the presence of the people of God in the world and the maintaining of biblical standards of moral purity?

(7)   What should be the Christian's primary concern while living in the world?

Integrity

The importance of integrity in the life of a believer cannot be overstated. Paul writes, *let everything you do reflect the integrity and seriousness of your teaching* (Titus 2:7 NLT). Integrity in one's life is fundamental to successfully merging matters of life and faith. The Christian is to live in a manner that inspires trust and confidence from others. Several components are involved in accomplishing this task.

First, there is the necessity of trust. The believer is to exemplify trustworthiness and dependability. This means one is to be a person of his/her word. Jesus states, *let your "Yes" be "Yes," and your "No," "No"; anything beyond this comes from the evil one* (Matthew 5:37). Trust is imperative if one is to impact others for Christ. Peter writes, *be careful to live properly among your unbelieving neighbors. Then even if they accuse you of doing wrong, they will see your honorable behavior* (I Peter 2:12, NLT).

Second, there is the necessity of spiritual fruit. The believer is to live in the Spirit, manifest the attitudes and actions of the Spirit, and refrain from pursuing the lusts of the flesh. *The Holy Spirit produces this kind of fruit in our lives: love, joy, peace, patience, kindness, goodness, faithfulness, gentleness, and self-control...Those who belong to Christ Jesus have nailed the passions and desires of their sinful nature to his cross and crucified them there* (Galatians 5:22-24, NLT).

Third, there is the necessity of possessing the character of Christ. Love for others is the qualifying trait of the Christian life. John writes, *let us continue to love one another, for love comes from God...This is real love—not that we loved God, but that he loved us and sent his Son as a sacrifice to take away our sins* (I John 4:7-10, NLT). The following questions provide guidelines for reflection:

(1)   What is the biblical definition of integrity?

(2)   Why is integrity essential for personal wholeness?

(3)   Why is integrity dependent upon true Christ-likeness?

(4)   How does one become Christ-like?

(5)   Is it possible to have a wholesome relationship with other people without integrity?

(6)   What are some examples of the kinds of problems one who tries to maintain integrity may encounter in the workplace?

(7)   How does integrity impact one's capacity to effectively evangelize the lost?

Self-Control

Self-control is a rare commodity in today's culture. Proverbs 16:32 states it is *better to have self-control than to conquer a city* (NLT). One of the primary benefits of our liberty in Christ is freedom from the domination of negative forces. Exemplary living calls for the believer to practice self-control in all areas of lifestyle and behavior. This involves several elements.

First, Paul compares self-control to being upright and holy. In the pastoral letters he writes of the need to be *self-controlled, upright, holy and disciplined* (Titus 1:8). Negative habits and addictions have no place among those who are living by a Christian ethic. This does not imply that one will never struggle with temptation. Nor does it imply that habits and addictions engrained over a period of time will immediately dissipate. It does suggest, however, that through the faithful and consistent application of Christian ethics, the power of Christ is available to break every habit, addiction, and bondage. Scripture clearly indicates that for the believer, *sin is no longer your master, for you no longer live under the requirements of the law. Instead, you live under the freedom of God's grace* (Romans 6:15).

Second, the believer is to consider the issue of behavior that is offensive to others. The Bible speaks clearly that one is to be sensitive to the needs and feelings of others. This allows one to demonstrate Christian love. It is true that a believer cannot please everyone in matters of lifestyle and behavior, nor should one seek to accommodate every whimsical non-biblical requirement imposed by others. However, *each of you should look not only to your own interests, but also to the interests of others* (Philippians 2:3-5). The following questions provide guidelines for reflection:

(1) What is the relationship between self-control and Christian discipleship?

(2) Why is a disciplined attitude more important to God than one's natural or acquired abilities?

(3) How does one maintain a disciplined attitude?

(4) Why should the Christian avoid vocabulary and conduct that are offensive to other people?

(5) Is there a relationship between gluttony, gambling and the use of drugs, alcohol or tobacco?

(6) How does drug addiction or alcoholism make it impossible to live under the complete Lordship of Christ?

(7) According to Romans 12:1-2, what is the biblical answer for all sinful practices?

Etiquette is defined as conduct or procedure required by good breeding or prescribed by authority to be observed in social or official life.[135] As it relates to exemplary living, etiquette may be understood as conduct or behavior prescribed by Christian ethics to be observed in one's daily life. It is a matter of protocol regarding the Christian life. This is accomplished by addressing three biblical subjects.

First, etiquette involves the subject of modesty. In this context, modesty is understood as a way of living that: 1) refrains from any action or activity that is unwholesome, impure, coarse, indecent or inappropriate; and 2) seeks to please God in all things. Paul writes, *live a life of love, just as Christ loved us and gave himself up for us as a fragrant offering and sacrifice to God* (Ephesians 5:2).

Second, etiquette involves the believer's manner of dress. The requirement of Christian ethics regarding one's manner of dress is not adherence to a particular style of clothing or the mandating of a specific piece of clothing. These vary between cultures and generations. The biblical requirement is modesty—that one's life and character are reflected in one's manner of dress. Regardless of the clothing type or style, one's manner of dress is to be modest. At this point, Paul's admonition is most helpful. *Do not conform to the pattern of this world, but...test and approve what God's will is—his good, pleasing and perfect will* (Romans 12:2).

Third, etiquette involves the subject of sensuality. Any conduct, behavior or manner of dress that intentionally draws attention to the carnal nature is sensual and violates biblical protocol. When one's conduct, behavior or manner of dress are suggestive, revealing or gratuitously extravagant, one is not demonstrating exemplary living. Paul writes, *live by the Spirit, and you will not gratify the desires of the sinful nature* (Galatians 5:16). The critical question at this point should be, "Is my conduct, behavior or manner of dress pleasing to Christ?" The following questions provide guidelines for reflection:

(1)   What is the biblical concept of modesty?

(2)   What fundamental relationship does the concept of modesty have with the Christian lifestyle?

(3)   What attitudes are prevalent in the church regarding modest appearance and the social trends of contemporary culture?

(4)   What is the biblical position regarding external adornment?

(5)   What is the biblical position on the clothing styles of the Christian?

(6)   How should the Christian determine his or her mode of dress?

(7)   What impact, if any, does the concept of modesty have on the mission of the church in the world?

Community

The axiom *no man is an island* is indeed true regarding Christian living. The body of Christ is no place for those who would live in seclusion. Believers are not to live in isolation with little or no access to the outside world. There is a social component of the Christian faith known as community. This is the framework in which salt, light, and yeast serve their purpose. Several aspects of community are important to understand.

First, living in a given culture requires participation in civil and social concerns. Christians are not exempt from this mandate. Paul writes, *everyone must submit to governing authorities. For all authority comes from God, and those in positions of authority have been placed there by God* (Romans 13:1). The only exception to this mandate is when civil law violates or is in opposition to the law of God. Apart from that, as a member of the community, the believer is to promote the well-being of the community at large. In so doing, the believer is engaging the culture for Christ.

Second, Christian ethics compels the believer to address inequality within the world. Contemporary culture is increasingly experiencing injustice, prejudice and oppression. Exemplary living compels the believer to constructively engage the needs of humanity. Jesus commends those who do so when he states, *I tell you the truth, whatever you did not do for one of the least of these, you did not do for me* (Matthew 25:45).

Third, Christian ethics involves protecting the weakest and most vulnerable within the community. At every opportunity, the believer's voice is to be heard regarding issues such as abortion or euthanasia. *Religion that God our Father accepts as pure and faultless is this: to look after orphans and widows in their distress* (James 1:27). The following questions provide guidelines for reflection:

(1) Should Christians have to choose between evangelism and community action, or can they engage in both?

(2) From a biblical standpoint, how can one justify the biblical concept that believers have a social obligation to fulfill?

(3) Should Christians be concerned about warfare?

(4) In what kind of situations, if any, would non-violent civil disobedience be the right course of action for a Christian?

(5) What are some specific ways in which Christians should be more actively involved in pursuing righteousness, justice and equity for all persons?

(6) What is the church called to do in the midst of the world in terms of its social obligations?

(7) How might the answer to question number 6 help the church to fulfill its mission of preaching the gospel?

The purpose of this chapter has been to present guidelines for promoting a Christian lifestyle. Beginning with the importance of a biblical worldview, this chapter then moved toward a merging of the theoretical and the practical. These guidelines are not presented as the *only* model for accomplishing the task of exemplary living but as *one* possible model. Each believer must not only ask but also give account for the answer to the question, "Does my life please God?"

CONCLUSION

This book explores the relationship between belief and behavior, specifically as it relates to the Christian lifestyle. Chapter 1 presents the results of a survey relating to the Christian lifestyle. In Chapter 2, the current context of the church, along with its challenges and opportunities is examined. Chapter 3 sets forth biblical foundations for the Christian life. In Chapter 4, a theological basis for Christian ethics is given. Chapter 5 offers an analysis of I Timothy 4:16 and its importance to Christian living. In Chapter 6, pursuing biblical guidelines is discussed. Chapter 7 focuses on how to live the Christian life. In Chapter 8, the merging of life and faith is illustrated.

The purpose of this book has not been to provide an exhaustive study of Christian ethics. Numerous works have been written on the subject. The purpose has not been to offer an exhaustive treatment regarding the various aspects of Christian lifestyle and behavior. Such a task would require volumes. The purpose has not been to implement a set of abrasive dictatorial rules for living. This has occurred far too many times. The purpose of this book has been to highlight the necessity of merging life and faith into a single journey—a journey of hope, grace, and victorious living. I trust that after reading the book you will have a renewed focus on Christian ethics, a renewed commitment to spiritual growth, and a renewed emphasis on a biblical lifestyle and behavior.

As you continue the process of merging life and faith, may our Lord grant you discernment and wisdom in all things.

ENDNOTES

1   George Barna, *The Index of Leading Spiritual Indicators* (Dallas: Word, 1996), 105.

2   George Barna, *The Second Coming of the Church* (Nashville: Word, 1998), 6.

3   Millard Erickson, *Postmodernizing the Faith* (Grand Rapids: Baker, 1998), 19.

4   Barna, Ibid., 1998, 6-7.

5   Ibid., 62.

6   Following is a sampling of the sources utilized: *The State of the Church: 2006*, a sixty-two-page document containing the most current statistical data from the Barna Research Group regarding the state of the American church; *Special report: The American Church in Crisis*, Rebecca Barnes and Lindy Lowry 2006, an article that polled prominent researchers and church leaders regarding church attendance trends in America; *Departure from God is Cause of America's Moral Decline*, Audrey Barrick 2007, a survey conducted in December 2006 by the Culture and Media Institute, that polled 2,000 Americans regarding moral issues

and the state of American society; *Slouching towards Gomorrah*, Robert Bork 1996, an enlightening volume regarding the decline of American values and morality. Bork traces this decline to the 1960's, a decade in which America's moral integrity experienced frontal assault, and from which the nation has never recovered; and, *The Next American Spirituality: Finding God in the 21st Century*, George Gallup 2000, offered relevant data regarding the state of spirituality in America.

7   The survey was comprised of an empirical study that included both qualitative and quantitative research. Probability sampling was used for the study, specifically, systematic random sampling via a survey. Probability sampling is well suited for research that utilizes surveys. Systematic random sampling spreads the sample more evenly over the target population.

8   Harvest Hills Church is an affiliate congregation of the Church of God (Cleveland, TN), located in Burlington, North Carolina.

9   Rick Warren, 2007, *Six Worldviews You're Competing Against,* Online article: http://www.christiantoday.com/article/rick.warren.six.worldviews.youre.competing.against/13420.htm. This article was adapted for use in the survey.

10   This section of the survey was adapted, http://www.churchofgod.org/practical-commitments.

11   Audrey Barrick, 2007, *Survey: Departure from God is Cause of America's Moral Decline,* Online article: http://www.christianpost.com/article/20070308/26212_Survey%3A_Departure_from_God_is_Cause_of_America%27s_Moral_Decline.htm.

12   Andy Crouch, "The Anti-Moderns," *Christianity Today,* November 2000, 76.

13   Charles Colson and Nancy Pearcey, *How Now Shall We Live?* (Nashville: Lifeway, 1999), 48.

14   Charles Dickens, *A Tale of Two Cities* (New York: Barnes & Noble, 2001), 1.

15   *The Sociology of Race and Ethnicity*, 2007, Online article: http://www.trinity.edu/mkearl/race.html.

16   Ellen Remmer, *What's a Donor to do? The State of Donor Resources in America Today* (Boston: The Philanthropic Initiative, 2000), 15.

17   George Gallup, *The Next American Spirituality: Finding God in the Twenty-First Century* (Colorado Springs: Cook, 2000), 33.

18   Robert Bork, *Slouching Towards Gomorrah: Modern Liberalism and American Decline* (New York: Regan Books, 1996), 251.

19   George Barna, *The Second Coming of the Church* (Nashville: Word, 1998), 55.

20   Gallup, Ibid, 62.

21   Walter Sundberg, *Religious Trends in Twentieth-Century America*, 2000, Online journal: http://www.luthersem.edu/word&world/Archives/20-1_20th_Century/20-1_Sundberg.pdf.

22   *Megachurches*, 2006, Online article: http://www.hirr.hartsem.edu/megachurch/megachurches.html.

23   George Barna, *The Index of Leading Spiritual Indicators* (Dallas: Word, 1996), 38.

24   R. Bliese, *Life on the Edge: A Small Church Redefines its Mission*, 2003, Online article: http://findarticles.com/p/articles/mi_m1058/is_14_120/ai105517536.

25   R. Barnes and L. Lowry, *Special Report: The American Church in Crisis*, 2006, Online article: http://www.christianitytoday.com/outreach/articles/americanchurchcrisis.html.

26   D. Olson, *The Future of the American Church from 2000-2010*, 2000, Online article: http://www.theamericanchurch.org/fut/fu6.htm.

27   Barna, Ibid., 1998, 16-17.

28   S. Thumma, D. Travis and W. Bird, *Mega-Churches Today*, 2005, Online article: http://hirr.hartsem.edu/megachurch/megastoday2005_summaryreport.html.

29   Ibid.

30   B. A. Robinson, *Trends Among Christians in the US*, 2006, Online article: http://www.religioustolerance.org/chr_tren.htm.

31   David Roozen, *Four Mega-Trends Changing America's Religious Landscape*, 2001, Online article: http://hirr.hartsem.edu/bookshelf/roozen_article4.html.

32   Gallup, Ibid, 50.

33   Roozen, Ibid.

34   Ibid.

35   George Barna, *The State of the Church: 2006* (Ventura: The Barna Group, 2006), 12-29.

36   Barna, 1998, Ibid, 6.

37   Douglas Groothuis, *Truth Decay* (Downers Grove: InterVarsity, 2000), 33.

38   Millard Erickson, *Postmodernizing the Faith* (Grand Rapids: Baker, 1998), 15.

39   Glendon Thompson, "Proclaiming the Gospel to Postmodernists" (Ph.D. diss., Potchefstroom University, 2000), 7.

40   Groothius, 34.

41   Erickson, Ibid, 16.

42   Thompson, Ibid, 10.

43   Ibid, 14-15.

44   Gallup, Ibid, 24.

45   Barna, Ibid, 59.

46   Thompson, Ibid, 38-39.

47   Gallup, Ibid, 42.

48   John Murray, *Principles of Conduct: Aspects of Biblical Ethics* (Grand Rapids: Eerdmans, 1957; reprint, 2001), 27 (page citations per the reprint edition).

49   Ibid, 202.

50   Henlee Barnette, *Introducing Christian Ethics* (Nashville: Broadman, 1998), 12.

51   Ibid, 19.

52   Wheeler Robinson, *Inspiration and Revelation in the Old Testament.* Westport: Greenwood Press, 1979), 241.

53   R. E. O. White, *Christian Ethics* (Macon: Mercer University Press, 1994), 22.

54   T. B. Maston, *Biblical Ethics* (Atlanta: Mercer University Press, 1997), 35.

55   Gordon McConville, *Exploring the Old Testament: A Guide to the Prophets*, vol. 4 (Downers Grove: InterVarsity Press, 2002), 202.

56   Barnette, Ibid., 13.

57   Frank Matera, *New Testament Ethics: The Legacies of Jesus and Paul* (Louisville: Westminster, 1996), 10.

58   George Ladd, *A Theology of the New Testament*, rev. ed., (Grand Rapids: Eerdmans, 1993), 126.

59   Samuel Mikolaski, *The Expositor's Bible Commentary*, vol. 1, (Grand Rapids: Zondervan, 1979), 477.

60   Barnette. Ibid., 44.

61   James Childress and John MacQuarrie, eds., *The Westminster Dictionary of Christian Ethics* (Philadelphia: Westminster, 1986), 421.

62   Ladd, Ibid., 522.

63   Barnette, Ibid., 73.

64   Edward Blaiklock, *The Expositor's Bible Commentary*, vol. 1, (Grand Rapids: Zondervan, 1979), 552.

65   Mikolaski, Ibid., 477.

66   F. F. Bruce, Romans, rev. ed., *Tyndale New Testament Commentaries*, vol. 6, (Grand Rapids: Eerdmans, 1985), 212.

67   Everett Harrison, Romans, *The Expositor's Bible Commentary*, vol. 10, (Grand Rapids: Zondervan, 1976), 126.

68   R. Alan Cole, Galatians, rev. ed., *Tyndale New Testament Commentaries*, vol. 9, (Grand Rapids: Eerdmans, 1989), 42.

69   N. T. Wright, Colossians and Philemon, *Tyndale New Testament Commentaries*, vol. 12, (Grand Rapids: Eerdmans, 1986), 133.

70   George Gallup, *The Next American Spirituality* (Colorado Springs: Cook, 2000), 32-34.

71   Verlyn Verbrugge, ed., *The NIV Theological Dictionary of the Bible* (Grand Rapids: Zondervan, 2000), 372.

72   Wayne Grudem, *Systematic Theology* (Grand Rapids: Zondervan, 1994), 26.

73   Samuel Mikolaski, *The Expositor's Bible Commentary*, vol. 1, (Grand Rapids: Zondervan, 1979), 477.

74   Frank Barackman, *Practical Christian Theology*, 3rd ed., (Grand Rapids: Kregel, 1998), 375.

75   Millard Erickson, *Christian Theology* (Grand Rapids: Baker, 1995), 1036.

76   Rodman Williams, *Renewal Theology*, 3 vols. in 1, (Grand Rapids: Zondervan, 1996), 299.

77   James Eckman, *Christian Ethics in a Postmodern World* (Wheaton: Evangelical Training Association, 1999), 6-8.

78   Lou Whitworth, *Measuring Morality: A Comparison of Ethical Systems*, Online article: http://www.leaderu.com/orgs/probe/docs/measmor.html, 1995.

79   Joseph Fletcher, *Situation Ethics: The New Morality* (Louisville: John Knox Press, 1997), 30.

80   Wayne Jackson, *A Critical Look at Situation Ethics*, Online article: http://www.christiancourier.com/articles/read/a_critical_look_at_situation_ethics, 1999.

81   George Barna, *The Second Coming of the Church* (Nashville: Word, 1998), 59.

82   Stanley Grenz, *The Moral Quest* (Downers Grove: InterVarsity, 1997), 17.

83   *Ethics and Morality*, Online article: http://www.seekingtruth.co.uk/morality_ethics.htm, 2008.

84   Whitworth, Ibid.

85   Roger Crook, *An Introduction to Christian Ethics,* 3rd ed., (Upper Saddle River: Preston Hall, 1999), 88.

86   Whitworth, Ibid.

87   *A Christian View of Ethics*, Online article: http://www.rapidresponsereport.com/technicalpapers.asp?ID=6, 2008.

88   Ibid.

89   *A Framework for Thinking Ethically*, Online article: http://www.scu.edu/ethics/practicing/decision/framework.html, 2008.

90   Jean-Jacques Rousseau, *The Social Contract* (New York: Penguin Books, 2004), 84.

91   Carl Henry, ed., *Baker's Dictionary of Christian Ethics* (Grand Rapids: Baker, 1981), 360-362. Adapted.

92   *A Christian View of Ethics*, Ibid.

93   Lawrence Becker and Charlotte Becker, eds., *Encyclopedia of Ethics,* 2nd ed., vol. II, (New York: Rutledge, 2001), 1187.

94   *A Christian View of Ethics*, Ibid. Adapted.

95   Henry, Ibid., 575.

96   *A Christian View of Ethics*, Ibid.

97   Fletcher, Ibid., 17-22.

98   *A Christian View of Ethics*, Ibid.

99   Gordon Fee, *New Testament Exegesis* (Philadelphia: Westminster, 1983), 21.

100   W. Vermillion, I Timothy, *Asbury Bible Commentary* (Grand Rapids: Zondervan, 1992), 1112.

101   Donald Guthrie, The Pastoral Epistles, rev. ed., *Tyndale New Testament Commentaries* (Grand Rapids: Eerdmans, 1990), 17.

102   Bruce Metzger, *The New Testament: It's Background, Growth, and Content*, 3rd ed., (Nashville: Abingdon, 2003), 240.

103   *The United Bible Society Greek New Testament*, UBS, 3rd ed., (Stuttgart, Germany: German Bible Society, 1975).

104   Guthrie, Ibid., 111.

105   Deborah Gill, The Pastorals, *Full Life Bible Commentary to the New Testament* (Grand Rapids: Zondervan, 1999), 1249.

106   Verlyn Verbrugge, *The NIV Theological Dictionary of New Testament Words* (Grand Rapids: Zondervan, 2000), 322-333.

107   James Dunn, The First and Second Letters to Timothy and the Letter to Titus, T*he New Interpreter's Bible*, vol. XI, (Nashville: Abingdon, 2000), 36.

108   George Barna, *The State of the Church: 2006* (Ventura: The Barna Group, 2006), 60.

109   Frank Barackman, *Practical Christian Theology*, 3rd ed., (Grand Rapids: Kregel, 1998), 376.

110   Millard Erickson, *Christian Theology* (Grand Rapids: Baker, 1995), 1056.

111   Barackman, Ibid, 424.

112   John Huffman, 2008, *Pentecost: Receiving God's Power Acts 2:1-47*. Online article: http://www.preaching.com/resources/sermons/11565753/page7/archive15/.

113   Paul Bucknell, 2008, *Matthew 5-7: The Sermon on the Mount*, Online article: http://www.foundationsforfreedom.net/References/NT/Gospels/Matthew/Matthew05-7_Outline.html. Portions of this article are adapted and incorporated in this section.

114   Alan Waltz, *A Dictionary for United Methodists*, (Nashville: Abingdon, 1991). Portions of this paragraph are adapted.

115   Verlyn Verbrugge, *The NIV Theological Dictionary of New Testament Words*. (Grand Rapids: Zondervan, 2000), 698.

116   French Arrington, The Pastorals, *Full Life Bible Commentary to the New Testament*, (Grand Rapids: Zondervan, 1999), 549.

117   Chuck Swindoll and Roy Zuck, *Understanding Christian Theology*, Nashville: Nelson, 2003), 1064.

118   F. Danker, *A Greek-English Lexicon of the New Testament and Other Early Christian Literature*, rev. ed., Chicago: University of Chicago Press, 2000), 552-553.

119   Richard Krejcir, *Doing Life Together*, Online article: http://sites.silaspartners.com/partner/Article_Display_Page/0,,PTID34418%7CCHID689934%7CCIID1875960,00.html, 2004.

120   Ibid.

121   Gerhard Kittel, *Theological Dictionary of the New Testament* (Vol II), (Grand Rapids: Eerdmans, 1964), 87-88.

122   Verbrugge, Ibid, 315.

123   Barackman, Ibid, 404.

124   Dan Kimball, *The Emerging Church*, Online article: http://www.inplainsite.org/html/the_emerging_church.html, 2007.

125   Mark Mittelberg, Lee Strobel and Bill Hybels, *Becoming a Contagious Christian: Communicating your Faith in a Style that Fits You*, rev. ed., (Grand Rapids: Zondervan, 1007), 51-65.

126   J. Rodman Williams, *Renewal Theology: Systematic Theology from a Charismatic Perspective* (3 vols in 1), (Grand Rapids: Zondervan, 1996), 90-101.

127   B. Liesch, *The New Worship: Straight Talk on Music and the Church*, (Grand Rapids: Baker Book House, 1996), 169.

128   Barackman, Ibid, 403.

129   Dick Eastman, *The Hour that Changes the World: A Practical Plan for Personal Prayer* (Grand Rapids: Chosen Books, 2005) 94.

130   Ibid, 96-101. Portions adapted.

131   Tobin Perry, *Ten Ways to Worship Without Music*, Online article: http://wtonline.ag.org/features/ten_ways_to_worship_without_music.cfm, 2008. Portions adapted.

132 Rick Warren, *Six Worldviews You're Competing Against*, Online article: http://www.christiantoday.com/article/rick.warren.six.worldviews.youre.competing.against/13420.htm, 2007.

133 George Barna, *The Second Coming of the Church*, (Nashville: Word, 1998), 144.

134 James Jenkins, *A Lifestyle to His Glory*, (Cleveland: Pathway, 1988.) Portions of this section are adapted from Jenkins' book.

135 *Webster's Ninth New Collegiate Dictionary*, (Springfield: Merriam-Webster Publishers, Inc., 1989), 427.

BIBLIOGRAPHY

A Christian View of Ethics. Online article: http://www. rapidresponsereport.com/technicalpapers.asp?ID=6, 2008.

A Framework for Thinking Ethically. Online article: http://www.scu. edu/ethics/practicing/decision/framework.html, 2008.

Arrington, French. The Pastorals. *Full Life Bible Commentary to the New Testament.* Grand Rapids: Zondervan, 1999.

Barackman, Frank. *Practical Christian Theology*, 3rd ed. Grand Rapids: Kregel, 1998.

Barna, George. *The Index of Leading Spiritual Indicators.* Dallas: Word, 1996.

_____. *The Second Coming of the Church.* Nashville: Word, 1998.

_____. *The State of the Church: 2006.* Ventura: The Barna Group, Ltd., 2006.

Barnes, Rebecca and Lindy Lowry. *Special Report: The American Church in Crisis.* Online article: http://www.christianitytoday.com/outreach/articles/americanchurchcrisis.html, 2006.

Barnette, Henlee. *Introducing Christian Ethics.* Nashville: Broadman, 1998.

Barrick, Audrey. *Survey: Departure from God is Cause of America's Moral Decline.* Online article: http://www.christianpost.com/article/20070308/26212_Survey%3A_Departure_from_God_is_Cause_of_America%27s_Moral_Decline.htm, 2007.

Becker, Lawrence and Charlotte Becker. *Encyclopedia of Ethics,* 2nd ed., Vol. II. New York: Routledge, 2001.

Blaiklock, Edward. The Epistolary Literature. *The Expositor's Bible Commentary,* Vol. 1. Grand Rapids: Zondervan, 1979.

Bliese, Richard. *Life on the Edge: A Small Church Redefines its Mission.* Online article: http://findarticles.com/p/articles/mi_m1058/is_14_120/ai105517536, 2003.

Bork, Robert. *Slouching Towards Gomorrah: Modern Liberalism and American Decline.* New York: Regan Books, 1996.

Bruce, F. F. Romans, Rev ed. *Tyndale New Testament Commentaries.* Grand Rapids: Eerdmans, 1985.

Bucknell, Paul. *Matthew 5-7: The Sermon on the Mount.* Online article: http://www.foundationsforfreedom.net/References/NT/Gospels/Matthew/Matthew05-7_Outline.html, 2008

Childress, James and John MacQuarrie. *The Westminster Dictionary of Christian Ethics.* Philadelphia: Westminster, 1986.

Cole, R. Alan. Galatians, Rev. ed. *Tyndale New Testament Commentaries.* Grand Rapids: Eerdmans, 1989.

Colson, Charles and Nancy Pearcey. *How Now Shall We Live?* Nashville: Lifeway, 1999.

Crook, Roger. *An Introduction to Christian Ethics*, 3rd ed. Upper Saddle River: Preston Hall, 1999.

Crouch, Andy. The Anti-Moderns. *Christianity Today*, Nov:76, 2000.

Danker, Frederick W. *A Greek-English Lexicon of the New Testament and Other Early Christian Literature,* Rev. ed. Chicago: University of Chicago Press, 2000.

Dickens, Charles. *A Tale of Two Cities*, Reprint. New York: Barnes & Noble Books, 2001.

Dunn, James. The First and Second Letters to Timothy and the Letter to Titus. *The New Interpreter's Bible,* Vol. XI. Nashville: Abingdon, 2000.

Eastman, Dick. *The Hour that Changes the World*. Grand Rapids: Chosen Books, 2005.

Eckman, James. *Christian Ethics in a Postmodern World*. Wheaton: Evangelical Training Association, 1999.

Erickson, Millard. *Christian Theology*. Grand Rapids: Baker, 1995.

_____. *Postmodernizing the Faith*. Grand Rapids: Baker, 1998.

Fee, Gordon D. *New Testament Exegesis*. Philadelphia: Westminster, 1983.

Fletcher, James. *Situation Ethics*, Reprint. Louisville: Knox Press, 1997.

Gallup, George Jr. *The Next American Spirituality*. Colorado Springs: Cook, 2000.

Gill, Deborah. The Pastorals. *Full Life Bible Commentary to the New Testament*. Grand Rapids: Zondervan, 1999.

Grenz, Stanley. *The Moral Quest*. Downers Grove: InterVarsity, 1997.

Groothuis, Douglas. *Truth Decay*. Downers Grove: InterVarsity, 2000.

Grudem, Wayne. *Systematic Theology: An Introduction to Biblical Doctrine*. Grand Rapids: Zondervan, 1994.

Guthrie, Donald. The Pastoral Epistles. Rev. ed. *Tyndale New Testament Commentaries*. Grand Rapids: Eerdmans, 1990.

Harrison, Everett. Romans. *The expositor's Bible Commentary*, Vol. 10. Grand Rapids: Zondervan, 1976.

Henry, Carl F. H. *Baker's Dictionary of Christian Ethics*. Grand Rapids: Baker, 1981.

Huffman John. *Pentecost: Receiving God's Power Acts 2:1-47*. Online article: http://www.preaching.com/resources/ sermons/11565753/page7/archive15/, 2008

Jackson, Wayne. *A Critical Look at Situation Ethics*. Online article: http://www.christiancourier.com/articles/read/a_critical_look_ at_situation_ethics, 1999.

Jenkins, James. *A Lifestyle to His Glory*. Cleveland: Pathway, 1988.

Kaiser, Walter. *Toward Old Testament Ethics*. Grand Rapids: Zondervan, 1983.

Kimball, Dan. *The Emerging Church*. Online article: http://www. inplainsite.org/html/the_emerging_church.html, 2007.

Kittel, Gerhard. *Theological Dictionary of the New Testament*, Vol. II. Grand Rapids: Eerdmans, 1964.

Krejcir, Richard. *Doing Life Together*. Online article: http://sites. silaspartners.com/partner/Article_Display_Page/0,,PTID34418 %7CCHID689934%7CCIID1875960,00.html, 2004

Ladd, George. *A Theology of the New Testament*, Rev. ed. Grand Rapids: Eerdmans, 1993.

Liesch, Barry. *The New Worship: Straight Talk on Music and the Church*. Grand Rapids: Baker, 1996.

Maston, Thomas B. *Biblical Ethics*, Reprint. Atlanta: Mercer University Press, 1997.

Matera, Frank. *New Testament Ethics: The Legacies of Jesus and Paul*. Louisville: Westminster, 1996.

McConville, Gordon. *Exploring the Old Testament*, Vol. 4. Downers Grove: InterVarsity, 2002.

Megachurches. Online article: http://www.hirr.hartsem.edu/ megachurch/megachurches.html, 2006.

Metzger, Bruce. *The New Testament: It's Background, Growth, and Content*, 3rd ed. Nashville: Abingdon, 2003.

Mikolaski, Samuel. The Theology of the New Testament. *The Expositor's Bible Commentary*, Vol. 1. Grand Rapids: Zondervan, 1979.

Mittelberg, Mark, Lee Strobel and Bill Hybels. *Becoming a Contagious Christian*, Rev. ed. Grand Rapids: Zondervan, 2007.

Murray, John. *Principles of Conduct: Aspects of Biblical Ethics*, Reprint. Grand Rapids: Eerdmans, 2001.

Olson, David. *The Future of the American Church from 2000-2010*. Online article: http://www.theamericanchurch.org/fut/fu6.htm, 2000

Perry, Tobin. *Ten Ways to Worship Without Music*. Online article: http://wtonline.ag.org/features/ten_ways_to_worship_without_music.cfm, 2008.

Practical Commitments. Online document: http://www.churchofgod.org/about/practical_commitments.cfm, 2007.

Remmer, Ellen. *What's a Donor to do? The State of Donor Resources in America Today*. Boston: The Philanthropic Initiative, 2000.

Robinson, B. A. *Trends Among Christians in the US*. Online article: http://www.religioustolerance.org/chr_tren.htm, 2006.

Robinson, Wheeler. *Inspiration and Revelation in the Old Testament*, Reprint. Westport: Greenwood Press, 1979.

Roozen, David. *Four Mega-Trends Changing America's Religious Landscape*. Online article: http://hirr.hartsem.edu/bookshelf/roozen_article4.html,2001.

Rousseau, Jean-Jacques. *The Social Contract*, Reprint. New York: Penguin Books, 2004.

Sundberg, Walter. *Religious Trends in Twentieth-Century America*. Online journal: http://www.luthersem.edu/word&world/Archives/20-1_20th_Century/20-1_Sundberg.pdf, 2000.

Swindoll, Charles and Roy Zuck. *Understanding Christian Theology*. Nashville: Nelson, 2003.

The Holy Bible, New American Standard Bible (NASB). Anaheim: Foundation, 1997.

The Holy Bible, New International Version (NIV). Colorado Springs: International Bible Society, 1973.

The Holy Bible, New Living Translation (NLT). Carol Stream: Tyndale, 1996.

The United Bible Society Greek New Testament, 3rd ed. Stuttgart: German Bible Society, 1983.

The Sociology of Race and Ethnicity. Online article: http://www.trinity.edu/mkearl/race.html, 2007

Thompson, Glendon. "Proclaiming the Gospel to Postmodernists." Ph.D. diss., Potchefstroom University, 2000.

Thumma, Scott, Dave Travis and Warren Bird. *Mega-Churches Today*. Online article: http://hirr.hartsem.edu/megachurch/megastoday2005_summaryreport.html, 2005

Verbrugge, Verlyn D. *The NIV Theological Dictionary of New Testament Words*. Grand Rapids: Zondervan, 2000.

Vermillion, W. I Timothy. *Asbury Bible Commentary*. Grand Rapids: Zondervan, 1992.

Williams, J. Rodman. *Renewal Theology*, 3 Vols. in 1. Grand Rapids: Zondervan, 1996.

Waltz, Alan. *A Dictionary for United Methodists*. Nashville: Abingdon, 1991.

Warren, Rick. *Six Worldviews You're Competing Against*. Online article: http://www.christiantoday.com/article/rick.warren.six.worldviews.youre.competing.against/13420.htm, 2007.

Webster's Ninth New Collegiate Dictionary. Springfield: Merriam-Webster Publishing, 1989

White, R. E. O. *Christian Ethics*. Macon: Mercer University Press, 1994.

Whitworth, Lou. *Measuring Morality: A Comparison of Ethical Systems.* Online article: http://www.leaderu.com/orgs/probe/docs/measmor.html, 1995.

Wright, N. T. Colossians and Philemon. *Tyndale New Testament Commentaries*, Vol. 12. Grand Rapids: Eerdmans, 1986.

39167865R00087

Made in the USA
Middletown, DE
08 January 2017